GLORIA STEWART

Being Joy™

A 40-DAY PROGRAM
to heal your life and
change the world

FriesenPress

Suite 300 - 990 Fort St
Victoria, BC, V8V 3K2
Canada

www.friesenpress.com

First Edition — 2018

ISBN
978-1-5255-3485-0 (Hardcover)
978-1-5255-3486-7 (Paperback)
978-1-5255-3487-4 (eBook)

1. SELF-HELP, PERSONAL GROWTH, HAPPINESS

Distributed to the trade by The Ingram Book Company

Table of Contents

Want more Joy in your life?

Joy is the highest-frequency emotion of all. It is an internal state of being and at the core of how you were always meant to be.

But many people have become detached and have forgotten what true joy feels like.

People are time stressed, nutrient starved, over-medicated, disease ridden, and disconnected from each other. They check out by turning to substances to dull their pain rather than discovering the root cause of their emptiness.

It's no wonder millions of people have lost hope that it can ever get better.

But it can.

Being Joy™ is a 40-day program to help you return to joy so that you can transform your life into medicine for a hurting world.

So, let's get started.

Gloria

Dedication

For all you noble citizens
who share this world with me
and want to make your meaning last
please listen to my plea.
Mother Earth weeps tears for us,
she feels our sickness growing.
Through anger, judgement, sadness blooms
and keeps our hearts from glowing.
She calls upon us, young and old
to heal our spirits, knowing
that joy remembered is joy returned,
your joy will keep life flowing.

Gloria

To My Beloved Reader,

Is joy the same as happiness? Is happiness the same as bliss? Is bliss the same as joy?

I asked myself these questions as I sat at my hotel desk to start this book. As I was staring out the window at the majestic mountains and forest that cocooned my room in the beautiful Kananaskis country of Alberta that busy Easter weekend, my tranquil thoughts were soon interrupted.

I noticed that I was becoming agitated by the sound of loud noises and laughter outside my door from the throngs of children and their families who had taken over the hotel for the holiday weekend. After a few minutes of quiet indignation, I suddenly realized that the sounds I was hearing were the sounds of joy. The children and the mountains had answered my question.

Joy is the feeling – the transformational juice that leads to all else. Without joy in your heart, there can be no bliss. In fact, joy is the highest frequency emotion there is.

Joy is an internal state of being and is at the core of how you and I were always meant to feel. Just like a child whose delight bubbles over in giddiness, the innocence and authenticity of joy lies within each of us. This book is my attempt to help you return to your natural state of joy and in so doing, change the world. Let me explain.

Our world is in turmoil. Read any newspaper or listen to the radio, nightly news, or internet story and you'll hear about homelessness, domestic violence, poverty, or the latest murder, suicide, world conflict, epidemic disease, and natural disaster. We live in a fear-based society and it's difficult to get away from the barrage of negativity.

People are time-stressed, nutrient-starved, over-medicated, disease-ridden, and disconnected from each other. They turn to substances like drugs, alcohol, food, sex, shopping, and gambling to dull their pain rather than discover the root cause of their emptiness. In fact, the global increase in the use of anti-anxiety medication and the alarming rise in depression, violence, and suicide cannot be taken lightly.

And physical diseases like cancer, chronic-fatigue syndrome, and fibromyalgia are common occurrences today – in large part due to minds, bodies, and spirits that are out of balance. It's no wonder that millions of people have lost hope that it will ever get better. But it can.

Being Joy is a book about hope – about remembering your joy and turning it into medicine for a sick world. This 40-day program, a movement actually, will take you on a magnificent journey of self-discovery and renewal.

I call it a movement because I truly believe that you and I have been called to heal the world through joy. As each one of us becomes more joyful, we will inspire those who will attract others and hence a movement is born – the Law of Attraction in perfect precision.

This book is divided into 40 chapters, each covering an important topic for each day of the program. You've likely heard that it takes about a month or so to form a new habit. I've settled on the number 40 as it has been the number I have personally used to make several major changes in my own life. In fact, in Rick Warren's best-selling book *The Purpose Driven Life,* he has listed several biblical references for how God used the power of 40 days to prepare people for important purposes. So, think of this as your very own Divine purpose – a "joyful habit" in the making.

My suggestion is that you follow the program for 40 consecutive days, reading each chapter in the morning along with the daily affirmation you'll find at the end of each chapter throughout the day. I've also included a daily activity to help reinforce the day's theme. At the end of each day spend a few minutes recording your thoughts and observations at the end of each chapter along with assessing your joy on the *Joy-meter*. You can repeat for another 40 days or simply open the book to a chapter that resonates with you after you have already completed the initial 40-day cycle.

My intention for this book is to assist you in living an amazingly joy-filled and abundant life. For as you increase the joy in your life, you will elevate your own vibrational frequency, which in turn will naturally intensify the power of your manifestations.

But remember, joy is a choice. If you want more joy, you need to *BE JOY.* Rediscover it for yourself. Your soul has been yearning for it. And it's been waiting for your return home.

Joyfully yours,

Gloria

P.S. I created a special 40-day card deck to accompany this book as a handy tool to reinforce your daily affirmations. Please see the back of this book for more details. Then get ready to be transformed.

"From joy all beings come,
in joy all beings live,
to joy all beings return."

~ Taittiriya Upanishad

Day 1

BE WORTHY

"Never forget that once upon a time,
in an unguarded moment,
you recognized yourself as a friend."

~ Elizabeth Gilbert

Why is it that most of us will go out of our way for others, but when it comes to ourselves, many say they feel like they're at the bottom of the priority list? Then they wonder why they feel exhausted – even resentful of the people they love the most?

I find this particularly true for many women today. I agree with Louise Hay who believes that the root of most of our problems in life is contained in the feeling *I'm not good enough*. When we have unconsciously set the bar so high for what makes a good mom, a good wife, a good friend, a good daughter, a good employee, or a good boss, it's no wonder that at the end of the day, the woman behind all those labels begins to feel inadequate and worse still – unworthy.

You see, the belief system of unworthiness, whether it is subtle or overt, leads to an inner state of victimhood. And when that takes hold, you worry about what's around the corner, and you look at the glass being half empty or even running out entirely. You see life as something that is happening to you rather than through you.

"Let's not forget that the little emotions are the great captains of our lives and we obey them without realizing it."

~ Vincent Van Gogh

We've all met people who just seem to attract disaster. They wonder why they have such "bad luck" – just can't seem to catch a break. But when we look at them more closely, we observe that they are chronic complainers, are easily offended by others, and are envious of what others have. All the while feeling an overwhelming sense of defeat that there is nothing they can do about it because that's just the way it is.

There are plenty of reasons why a state of unworthiness might exist such as not feeling like we measure up to what society expects.

Some of this is adopted as we mature and begin to perpetuate beliefs that validate life experiences we have already had – *This happened to me before and it will happen again. I just have bad luck. I must not be good enough.*

Others suffer from poor self-worth because of family upbringing or other negative situations in their lives, which occurred in their formative years as they were learning to define themselves.

And some people fall into victimhood as a result of "imprinting." Stay with me on this one for a minute.

I had a brother who passed away a few years ago. He was the epitome of a person living as a victim, however, I never understood what caused him to believe that until recently.

There were three kids in our family – I am the eldest. We grew up in an average, middle-class family. Our home-life was nurturing, stable, and supportive. We had parents who loved each other dearly and there was always love and laughter in our home. So why would one child feel so unworthy while the other two did not?

My brother just seemed to be one of those people who attracted "bad luck." If something was going to happen, it was going to happen to him. It went from injuries, to accidents, to vehicles breaking down, to people taking advantage of him, and eventually to serious illness, cancer, and death at fifty-seven years old. We were never surprised by some of the things that happened to him as they seemed to be par for the course. Even at his death, sadly we were not surprised. So, here's what I have learned and want to share with you.

For the past several years I have been more and more interested in metaphysics, and I have worked closely with people in the energy-healing and shamanic field. What I learned about "imprinting" was revealing and it gave me such a great feeling of peace about my brother's life-long behaviours.

You see, when my mother was pregnant with my brother, her mother died – at the young age of fifty-two. Her father had died only the year before, so my mom was in a pretty bad place when she lost her beloved mother. I remember her telling me that she had always had a strong faith in God, but because "God took away both my parents so early," she was angry at God and began to question why this was "happening to me." This energy imprinted onto my brother while he was in-vitro.

That explained so much. You see, the energy of those feelings of victimhood that my mother felt so strongly while carrying my brother, left a life-long imprint on his entire being. I can remember him as a small boy and knowing what I know now, I can see how that imprint revealed itself in his early life.

Now that's not to say that he couldn't have shifted from that energy by doing some release work with a trained professional, but unfortunately, I only discovered this for myself recently.

So, if you or someone you know struggles with feelings of unworthiness and victimhood, then please don't wait those feelings completely dominate your life. There is so much that you can do about it.

"At the center of your being you have the answer; you know who you are and you know what you want."
~ Lao Tzu

For starters, just acknowledging that you feel this way is the most important step. And recognize that you are not alone. In fact, it's quite the epidemic.

Then if you haven't already, start to read about the Law of Attraction and how your vibrational frequency affects everything in your life. There are so many useful resources for this subject that I'm not going to elaborate on this too much here, but I encourage you to begin that journey of self-discovery as soon as you can.

And as you will discover in every chapter of this book, the best method I've found to create more joy and happiness is to *be the feeling* that you most want to be.

For example, if you aren't feeling sure of yourself at the moment and are in a place of lack and fear, then just repeat the statement, "I AM WORTHY" every time those thoughts cross your mind. You have that power – you have that ability to shift your reality by changing your thoughts about yourself. Trust me. You are worthy. You are enough. And you are deserving of anything that your heart desires. And that is joyful living.

Day 1

MY DAILY AFFIRMATION

The sky lit up when I was born,
the heavens opened wide.
That I am here to take my place
serves all of us with pride.

MY DAILY ACTIVITY

WORRY STONE: Find a nice stone or crystal such as citrine, rose quartz, or clear quartz that you can carry in your pocket or have near you all day long. When you notice that you are feeling anxious about something or are doubting your self-worth, touch your stone or crystal, breathe deeply, smile, give yourself a big hug, and say out loud, *"I am worthy just the way I am."*

MY DAILY FREQUENCY SHIFTER

At the end of each day, rate your state of joy on this **Joy-meter** *and then make any comments or observations about your feelings during the day or about anything noteworthy that occurred. This will help you see how your joy increases during the 40 days and what "shows up" for you.*

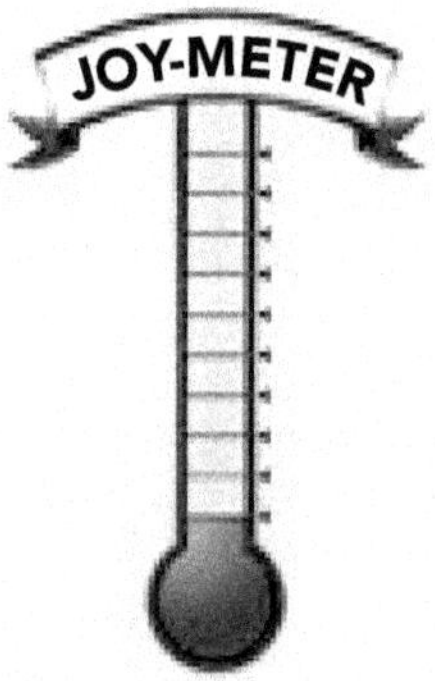

10 – Off the charts.
9 – Super amazing.
8 – Pretty blissful.
7 – Oh happy joy.
6 – I believe.
5 – I've turned the corner.
4 – I'm breathing easier.
3 – I can see the light.
2 – The clouds are lifting.
1 – I feel depressed.

NOTES

Day 1

MORE NOTES

Day 2

BE OF SERVICE

"I slept and dreamt that life was joy.
I awoke and saw that life was service.
I acted and behold, service was joy."

~Rabindranath Tagore

I love the subject of service. As far as I'm concerned, it's one of the most direct paths to joy.

But for me, service is not just about giving time or money in an organized way to causes or projects you believe in. Of course, being of service to the greater good is extremely important. Many an organization would cease to exist if it weren't for the countless volunteers and financial supporters who serve the varied needs of humankind. I have spent the better part of thirty years consulting in the social-purpose sector, where I have come to understand and respect our collective responsibility to the evolution of civil society throughout the world.

But I think of "service" in a much more fundamental way than that. To me, true service is about being fully engaged and present when we are in the company of another.

To be of true service we must give one hundred percent of ourselves so that the other person knows that they are of value – that they are worthy. And of course, when we do that, the law of reciprocity kicks in and we in turn are served as well.

So how can we best demonstrate our full engagement to others? Well, I think the best way is to cultivate good, heart-centered listening abilities.

"Silent" and "listen" are spelled with the same letters.

Have you ever been in a conversation with someone who you know has not been listening to what you've said? Instead they were already preparing what they were going to say next, or worse still, they interrupted you to have their own say. *(I know – we've all done it.)* Frustrating isn't it? Whether this person politely listened or not, you know he or she has not really heard you.

How does that make you feel? I've even had this happen during phone calls, where I know I could have put the phone down, walked away for a few minutes, and returned to the person still having a conversation all by him or herself.

Next time that happens, just stop for a minute. Become silent and listen. Tune into the situation. Is this a person who just needs someone to hold space for them as they express their feelings? If that's the case, then be there for them.

Now, I don't mean that you should take on their problems. That won't serve either one of you. There's a difference between being empathetic and being sympathetic. Listen intently with compassion and sincerity. Be present. Honour their humanity. Listen with your heart.

> ***"Listening moves us closer, it helps us become more whole, more healthy, more holy. Not listening creates fragmentation, and fragmentation is the root of all suffering."***
> ~ Margaret J. Wheatley

Time after time I've found that if I'm starting to feel a bit sorry for myself or if my personal frequency is low, the best way to shift is to surrender and give myself away. I can do it either silently without the other person even knowing or I can serve love in a more public way by picking up the phone or writing them an email or better still – a letter, to tell them how much I value them in my life.

Expressing your feelings is an act of caring about another. And listening as they express theirs is a sacred demonstration of service to the universe.

So, I ask you to say aloud – *"How may I serve?"* And then say, *"Thank you."* For to be of service is to be served. And that is joyful living.

Day 2

MY DAILY AFFIRMATION

Today as I wake
I ask, how may I serve?
For to give from my heart
sends back all I deserve.

MY DAILY ACTIVITY

GIVE WITHOUT EXPECTATION: Do something nice for a family member or co-worker today without expectation. Or make an anonymous donation to a cause you care about. The point of the activity is to be of service to others, without the expectation of a thank you.

MY DAILY FREQUENCY SHIFTER

At the end of each day, rate your state of joy on this **Joy-meter** *and then make any comments or observations about your feelings during the day or about anything noteworthy that occurred. This will help you see how your joy increases during the 40 days and what "shows up" for you.*

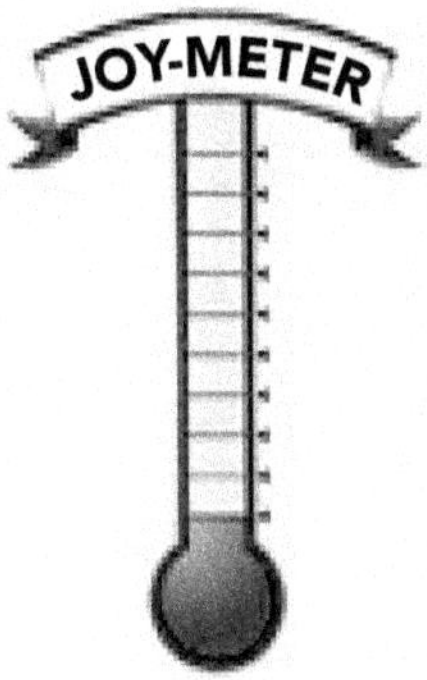

10 – Off the charts.
9 – Super amazing.
8 – Pretty blissful.
7 – Oh happy joy.
6 – I believe.
5 – I've turned the corner.
4 – I'm breathing easier.
3 – I can see the light.
2 – The clouds are lifting.
1 – I feel depressed.

NOTES

Day 2

Day 3

BE INSPIRED

"Materialism is a circumference without a centre.
Idealism is a centre without a circumference."

~Augustus William Hare and Julius Charles Hare

Having ideals that you are prepared to live up to and daring to dream big dreams are one and the same as far as I'm concerned. It all starts from that burning desire inside you – the inspiration – that says, this is what I am passionate about. This is what gives meaning to my life and this is my truth. Then putting those ideals into action to spark change in our world is what it's all about.

Think about the many famous artists, inventors, and scientists who had they not been serial idealists, would not have had the vision and passion to create. They were not afraid to dream big, to let inspiration take hold, and to let their ideals and passion fuel their actions for turning dreams into reality. Our world has been greatly enriched because they were inspired – "in spirit" and living in a state of joy.

Idealists are change agents – the true mavericks of society. They learn the rules, so they can break them properly. But being an idealist does not come without its challenges.

Idealists are often targeted as having "their heads in the clouds" or being "unrealistic" or my personal favourite – "too idealistic." What does that even mean – "too idealistic"?

"I am always grateful for the idea that used me."

~ Alfred Adler

Idealists don't just go along with the status quo. They are usually insulated from what Deepak Chopra calls "the hypnosis of social conditioning." They follow their own path and do it their way. And in my opinion, adopting an idealistic outlook leads to a more accountable life, not a less accountable one.

I've found that idealists are less likely to feel unworthy or behave like victims. They understand, as Joe Vitale puts it in his book, *Zero Limits*, that "intention is a toy of the mind. Inspiration is a directive from the Divine." They tap into that Divine source of inspiration and act upon their ideas and the ideals that shape them.

If you can relate to this, then you're not alone. Don't apologize for being an idealist and please do not stifle your individuality. Be proud. And pledge to do things that improve the human condition in your own unique way. It's what our planet depends on.

But if you do not consider yourself an idealist – if your life has been more pragmatic, I would like to challenge you for a minute.

> ***"When you are inspired by some great purpose, some extraordinary project, all of your thoughts break their bonds. Your mind transcends limitations, your consciousness expands in every direction, and you find yourself in a new, great, and wonderful world. Dormant forces, faculties, and talents become alive and you discover yourself to be a greater person by far than you ever dreamed yourself to be."***
> ~ Patanjali

Look around for the multitude of examples of what inspiration and idealism have created in our world. Everything you see is because of someone's imagination and the actions that were taken to bring them about.

I believe, at our core, we are all idealists. We have ideals about how we see the world – and they are all unique, just as we are all unique. For we see the world not as it is, but as we are. Therefore, we are all idealists. Follow my logic?

The thing is that not all of us act on our ideals, especially if they are different from that of the "tribe." Most of the time, that's because of fear of being ostracized, or of standing out or making waves. But waves are good. They inspire us and others. That's how change happens.

"When you're inspired you activate dormant forces and the abundance you seek in any form comes streaming into your life."

~ Wayne Dyer

So today as you experience the many blessings that idealism has brought our world, look deep inside to find your "inner rebel." Tell him or her it's safe to come out and play. In fact, it's downright fun. And that is joyful living.

Day 3

MY DAILY AFFIRMATION

When I'm inspired my heart beats faster.
I feel alive and new.
Because I know I'm my own master,
I follow what is true.

MY DAILY ACTIVITY

WHO INSPIRES YOU? Research and read about someone you admire who inspires you. List the qualities you admire about them and what you could do to emulate those characteristic. Then celebrate as you begin to inspire others.

MY DAILY FREQUENCY SHIFTER

At the end of each day, rate your state of joy on this ***Joy-meter*** *and then make any comments or observations about your feelings during the day or about anything noteworthy that occurred. This will help you see how your joy increases during the 40 days and what "shows up" for you.*

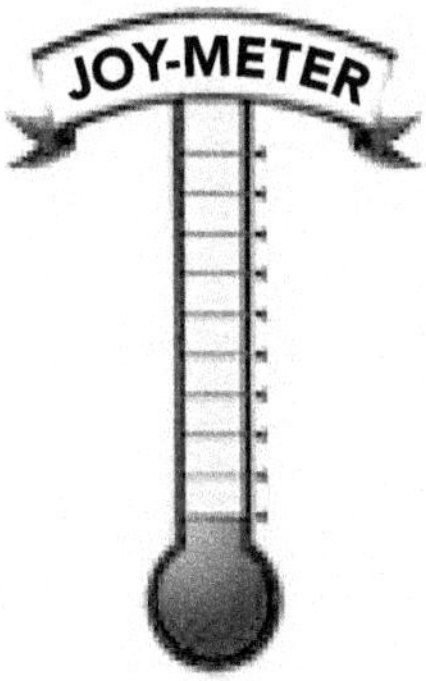

10 – Off the charts.
9 – Super amazing.
8 – Pretty blissful.
7 – Oh happy joy.
6 – I believe.
5 – I've turned the corner.
4 – I'm breathing easier.
3 – I can see the light.
2 – The clouds are lifting.
1 – I feel depressed.

NOTES

Day 3

Day 4

BE SMILEY

*"Let my soul smile through my heart
and my heart smile through my eyes,
that I may scatter rich smiles in sad hearts."*

~Paramahansa Yogananda

I know I always feel better when I smile. So, thanks to a little website I found called Nature's Blessings, I learned that when we smile we actually contract fifteen muscles on our faces and move 230 muscles out of the 630 muscles we have in our entire bodies.

According to Dr. William Fry of Stanford University, smiling stimulates the human brain to release chemicals that inhibit infection and lessen pain. Smiling is not only the best brain exercise, it also increases blood circulation and heart rate. Four minutes of smiling has the same effect as an upper-body workout. And five minutes of smiling is better than a five-hour work out. Wow – beats the treadmill as far as I'm concerned.

But I think, perhaps best of all, when you are smiling, you can't feel angry, sad, or fearful, which are all low-vibration energies that play havoc with your immune system and overall sense of wellbeing. Simply put, smiling brings joy, and joy heals.

"Sometimes your joy is the source of your smile, but sometimes your smile can be the source of your joy."

~Thich Nhat Hanh

Do you remember the 2010 movie, *Eat, Pray, Love,* which was based on the best-selling book of the same name by Elizabeth Gilbert? There was a great scene in the movie when Julia Roberts was learning to meditate in India. Like so many people new to meditation, she found it challenging to quiet the mind and just be. Ketut Leyir, her teacher said:

"To meditate, only you must smile. Smile with face, smile with mind, and good energy will come to you and clear away dirty energy. Even smile in your liver."

I loved that scene in the movie and that quote really stuck with me. But you don't have to wait to meditate to be in a smiling place. Just practice smiling more at work, while driving your car, or when you're making dinner. *(That's a really important time to smile as you'll be transferring your good energy to the food you prepare and take into your body.)*

Another thing. Have you ever noticed that smiles are contagious? Try this experiment:

Next time you see a stranger on the street or at the bank or grocery check-out, just smile. Exercise those face muscles. Chances are the person will smile back. It's like a mirror — just like when new babies imitate their moms or dads when first learning to smile. Sometimes, we just have to teach others. But we first need to teach ourselves. Remember, we can't give away what we don't already have. So, smile, smile, smile.

"Let us always meet each other with smile, for the smile is the beginning of love."
~ Mother Teresa

Practice smiling today. You'll raise your own frequency and send love to all those you meet. You'll radiate an energy that will draw in other people. You'll be sharing your joy with the world. And that is joyful living.

Day 4

MY DAILY AFFIRMATION

My eyes are wide and bright.
My mouth smiles, "I see you."
My heart expands
as love commands
for Spirit sees me too.

MY DAILY ACTIVITY

SMILE, SMILE, SMILE. Today, make a point of smiling at everyone you meet. And if you're alone today, just smile at yourself – while you sit, while you read, work, and prepare meals. And especially when you look at yourself in the mirror.

MY DAILY FREQUENCY SHIFTER

At the end of each day, rate your state of joy on this **Joy-meter** *and then make any comments or observations about your feelings during the day or about anything noteworthy that occurred. This will help you see how your joy increases during the 40 days and what "shows up" for you.*

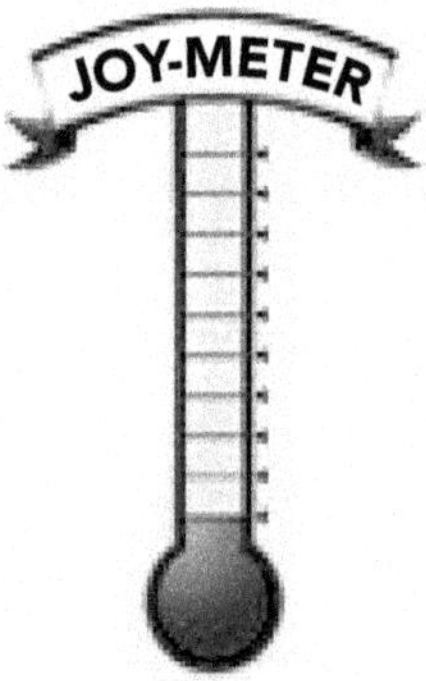

10 – Off the charts.
9 – Super amazing.
8 – Pretty blissful.
7 – Oh happy joy.
6 – I believe.
5 – I've turned the corner.
4 – I'm breathing easier.
3 – I can see the light.
2 – The clouds are lifting.
1 – I feel depressed.

NOTES

Day 4

MORE NOTES

Day 5

BE GENTLE

"Nothing is so strong as gentleness.
Nothing is so gentle as real strength."

~ St. Francis de Sales

Today I am having a gentle day — quiet; a time for reading and calm. A day to surround myself with gentle energy, nourish my body with gentle food, and speak lovingly to myself and others. A time to nurture my inner strength through gentleness.

I believe the world needs this collective strength through gentleness now more than ever. And we should be honouring those who are gentle and sensitive rather than perceiving them as weak.

When I think of the word gentle, the first person who comes to my mind is my father. And I'm not the only one who thinks this way.

At my father's funeral a few years ago, I described him this way in my eulogy – as a gentleman – a gentle man. Many a person came up to me that day to tell me stories of what a "gentle" man he was. Those are the memories I choose to keep. He was gentle and yet he was strong.

All the men in our family are gentle and sensitive; my son, my two brothers, and my two nephews. But quite frankly I never really understood gentleness from the standpoint of strength until I read that quote of St. Francis de Sales. It makes sense to me now. Here's why.

A gentle man (or woman, of course) is first and foremost sensitive. Sensitive to their own physical, emotional, and spiritual needs. And mindful of the energies of others. They are compassionate, choose not to be confrontational for the sake of confrontation, and have great empathy for the world around them. They know how to love and that is where their strength comes from. Therefore, their strength enables their gentleness. And they live with an abundance of joy in their hearts.

***"Gentleness is the strength behind true power and it comes from feeding yourself with nourishing words, thoughts,
deeds, intentions
and all forms of food."***
~ Doreen Virtue

Today, as we listen to stories of school violence and watch while many of our world's leaders fight for power as they bully each other, it's important to remember that they don't do this from a position of strength but of insecurity. And when more of us realize this, we can send them love instead of hatred and rather than judgement – understanding.

I call out now to our entire planet's mothers and fathers to love their sons and daughters by teaching them gentleness. I believe that is the only way our world can heal. And that is joyful living.

Day 5

MY DAILY AFFIRMATION

Soft and gentle to myself
I soothe the inner fire.
As calm resumes
love consumes.
I'm safe within desire.

MY DAILY ACTIVITY

PURIFY AND SOOTHE THE SOUL: Honour gentleness and sensitivity today by eating healthy, fresh food. Drink more water. Reduce the amount of time you spend on the computer or cell phone or watching TV. Live today in a state of honouring your innate gentle nature. Be soft. Speak quietly, listen to soothing music, surround yourself with gentle people, or be alone today. Walk slowly. Allow gentleness to be your state of being for the day.

MY DAILY FREQUENCY SHIFTER

At the end of each day, rate your state of joy on this **Joy-meter** *and then make any comments or observations about your feelings during the day or about anything noteworthy that occurred. This will help you see how your joy increases during the 40 days and what "shows up" for you.*

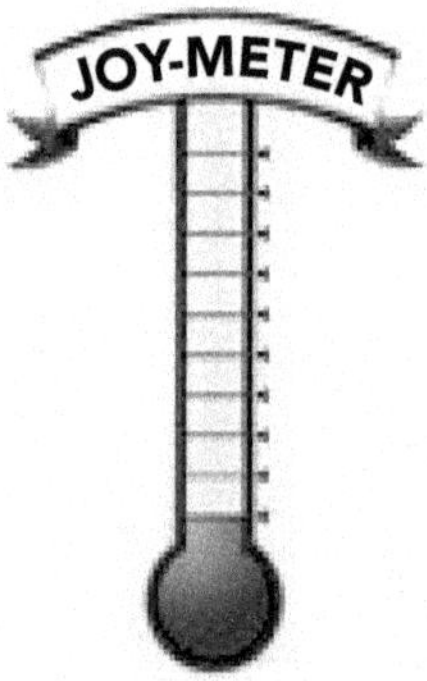

10 – Off the charts.
9 – Super amazing.
8 – Pretty blissful.
7 – Oh happy joy.
6 – I believe.
5 – I've turned the corner.
4 – I'm breathing easier.
3 – I can see the light.
2 – The clouds are lifting.
1 – I feel depressed.

NOTES

Day 5

MORE NOTES

Day 6

BE OPTIMISTIC

"There are two ways to live your life.
One is as though nothing is a miracle.
The other is as though everything is a miracle."

~ Albert Einstein

I've sometimes been told that I'm naïve, too impressionable, not a realist – usually by people close to me who are concerned that I'm setting myself up for disappointment. But I've always been an optimist – one of the most essential qualities for joy I believe.

From my earliest memories, I emulated the little girl from the book *Pollyanna*. I related to her on a level that was deep and to my core. Like Pollyanna I knew there was always a silver lining and that everyone should be given the benefit of the doubt. That belief has certainly been put to the test many times in my life.

However, I knew that every set-back was a learning experience and moved me closer to where I longed to be, even if at times I wasn't entirely sure where that was. I believed then and still do today, that every person, place, and event I've experienced has meaning and has shaped the human being I am today. And at the foundation of that has always been an optimism that energizes and propels me to get up each time I fall and to do the cha-cha rather than lie down in defeat.

"Optimist: someone who figures that taking a step backward after taking a step forward is not a disaster, it's a cha-cha."

~Robert Brault

You see my optimism comes from a knowing that we co-create our own destiny. That the choices we make and the thoughts we think have everything to do with the outcome.

And like Pollyanna, because I believe in the power of good, I see more good than evil. Because I believe that I am responsible for my own joy, I am more joyful than sad. And because I am an optimist, I am simply more at peace with events as they unfold around me – there are no mistakes and everything that happens has meaning and purpose, even if I can't see it at the time.

But, you ask, what about all the problems in the world today? Political instability, poverty, homelessness, violence, environmental contamination. How can I feel optimistic about a future with all that to worry about?

So, here's the deal about fear. When you're in fear, you can't hear. And fear blocks joy. When you are fearful and fret about things, you create resistance, and that restricts the flow of possibility. Put simply, when you worry, you let fear drive the decisions you make and that has a decided impact on the amount of joy you feel, which slows down your ability to manifest what you want. Remember – joy is your opportunity magnet.

> ***"No matter what it is, if you really want it, and if you get out of the way of it, it will happen. It must be. It is Law. It can be no other way. It's the way this Universe is established. If you want it and relax, it will happen."***
> ~Abraham-Hicks

Still need some inspiration to shift your perspective? Well a terrific book I ran across that might help you dissolve any pessimistic views you hold about the future is called *Abundance: The Future is Better Than You Think,* by Peter H Diamandis and Steven Kotler. These authors epitomize optimism and have provided some great evidence for a future we should all get excited about.

Another great resource to inspire you about the possible, is a magazine called *The Intelligent Optimist.* Published in the Netherlands, this magazine has a growing international following of people like me, who believe that optimism will prevail and that we, as a global community can successfully work together to resolve issues and change the face of our future. I encourage you to look at it. A steady diet of inspiration from resources like these can do wonders to shift the energy you attach to events and situations in your daily life.

"Infinite riches are all around you if you can open your mental eyes and behold the treasure house of infinity within you. There is a gold mine within you from which you can extract everything you need to live life gloriously, joyously, and abundantly.

~ Joseph Murphy

This world has plenty of examples of optimism at work – for healing and for joy. Look around to find your own examples. Deepak Chopra said it best: *"You must find the place inside yourself where nothing is impossible."* And when you find it, celebrate and share your joy with others. Then join me in a "cha-cha" anytime you stumble. And that is joyful living.

Day 6

MY DAILY AFFIRMATION

Today my thoughts will only be
in knowing that I hold the key
for having what I wish to see
because my heart believes in me.

MY DAILY ACTIVITY

DECLARE A COMPLAINT-FREE DAY. Complaining can be a habit. So, today begin to break that habit. Make a practice of catching yourself when you start to complain about anything and instead smile and say, "All is well." Eventually things and people that used to irritate you will stop showing up in your life.

MY DAILY FREQUENCY SHIFTER

At the end of each day, rate your state of joy on this **Joy-meter** *and then make any comments or observations about your feelings during the day or about anything noteworthy that occurred. This will help you see how your joy increases during the 40 days and what "shows up" for you.*

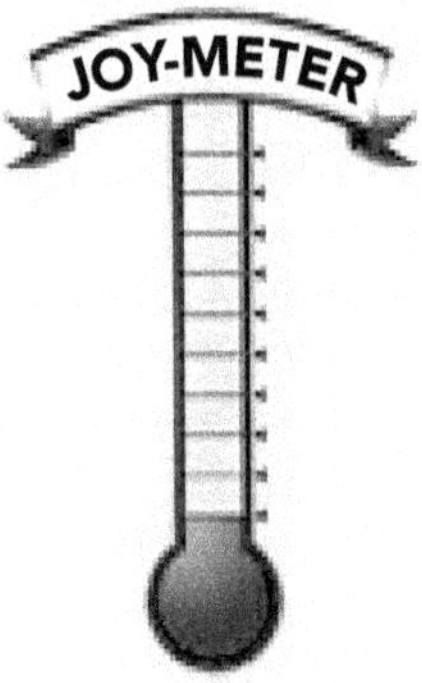

10 – Off the charts.
9 – Super amazing.
8 – Pretty blissful.
7 – Oh happy joy.
6 – I believe.
5 – I've turned the corner.
4 – I'm breathing easier.
3 – I can see the light.
2 – The clouds are lifting.
1 – I feel depressed.

NOTES

Day 6

Day 7

BE ENTHUSIASTIC

"Every great and commanding movement
in the annals of the world
is due to the triumph of enthusiasm.
Nothing great was ever achieved without it."

~ Ralph Waldo Emerson

Did you know that the word "enthusiasm" comes from the Greek word "enthousiasmos," which consists of the root words "theos" (god) and "en" (in)? It literally means "The God Within."

I find this to be quite profound. To me, this means that the excitement you feel through your enthusiasm in something is at the very core of your being – your life force, if you will.

So, if you're not living in the bright light of love for everything around you, then you're living in the low energy of apathy. A life-force that is dim and depleted. Not a place that will attract opportunity or abundance. Not a place you want to stay.

Today, more than ever, our world needs more enthusiasm and less doom and gloom. If you don't like where you are, you need to change it. But you can't do that if you're stuck in your comfort zone. You'll only continue to feel lethargic or defeated.

So how can you get more enthused about something? How can you dig yourself out of apathy?

"It's faith in something and enthusiasm for something that makes a life worth living."

~ Oliver Wendell Holmes, Sr.

Start small. Pick one thing, that when you think of it, you smile. A beloved family member or friend. Your pet. Perhaps a favourite book or movie. A restaurant you like to go to. A great vacation you've had. Just close your eyes and think of that one thing.

Does it make you smile?

Now think of another thing that brings you joy. How does it make you feel? Can you feel your energy starting to shift? Not yet? Then close your eyes and let yourself drift, all the while imagining something – just one thing that you can feel excited about. That's the first step.

Now that your energy has started to shift you into a place of appreciation and joy, you'll find that momentum will begin to mobilize you into activities that best express your enthusiasm. You'll feel less depleted and more energized as you move closer to fulfilling your desires.

> ***"Enthusiasm is not the same as just being excited. One gets excited about going on a roller coaster. One becomes enthusiastic about creating and building a roller coaster."***
> ~ Bo Bennett

Let this be your call to action. Get enthused about something today. In fact, I challenge you to get giddy with it. Feel the energy pulse through your veins. Practice joy and let that be your fuel. Then you know what's going to happen? Your enthusiasm will act as a magnet for more joy.

Norman Vincent Peale said it best, *"There is a real magic in enthusiasm. It spells the difference between mediocrity and accomplishment."*

So be the joy. Shift your energy and help our world in the process. And that is joyful living.

Day 7

MY DAILY AFFIRMATION

Energy is pulsing
throughout my heart and veins.
Excitement for the day ahead.
Joy is my own domain.

MY DAILY ACTIVITY

MAKE A JOY BOARD: You've probably heard about vision boards for helping manifest things you want to show up in your life. Today, make a Joy Board that represents all the feelings, things, or people that bring you joy now and in the future. As you cut out pictures and paste them onto a board or scrapbook, feel your enthusiasm increase as you shift your frequency with joyful thoughts.

MY DAILY FREQUENCY SHIFTER

At the end of each day, rate your state of joy on this **Joy-meter** *and then make any comments or observations about your feelings during the day or about anything noteworthy that occurred. This will help you see how your joy increases during the 40 days and what "shows up" for you.*

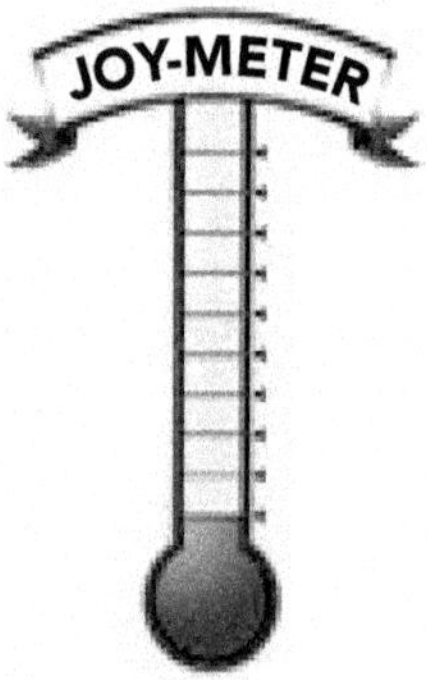

10 – Off the charts.
9 – Super amazing.
8 – Pretty blissful.
7 – Oh happy joy.
6 – I believe.
5 – I've turned the corner.
4 – I'm breathing easier.
3 – I can see the light.
2 – The clouds are lifting.
1 – I feel depressed.

NOTES

MORE NOTES

Day 8

BE RELEASED

"When I let go of what I am,
I become what I might be.
When I let go of what I have,
I receive what I need."

~ Tao Te Ching

This is such a huge subject and one that is so incredibly important for living a joyful life. So, I'm going to embark a little more upon the metaphysical domain for this chapter as I believe it's integral to your understanding of how "release" leads to joy.

Perhaps the best example is one you've likely already had in your life. We've all experienced the frustration of misplacing an item. Perhaps your car keys – you search the house in earnest, looking under and over things, feeling anxious and panicky while you search in vain.

Or perhaps you are trying to remember the name of a movie or book and it's like right on the tip of your tongue, but the more you try to remember the more frustrated you become.

Then a little while later, it's like bingo – you remember the movie or book title or where you left the keys. Once you take your attention off the "problem" the solution can appear. It's the attention to the problem that keeps the struggle going.

When you intentionally let go of your attachment to finding or remembering the thing and instead relax, then the solution is more available to you. I know it sounds counter-intuitive but that's really how it works.

It might feel like a random happening that you suddenly remember, but in reality, it's the Law of Attraction at work. You see, what you focus on is what is drawn to you, so when you're thinking "lost" or "can't remember" or "lack" or whatever, that's what the Universe sends back to you. Just like a magnet, you are attracting what you think about whether you want it or not.

"By letting go all gets done."
~ Lao Tzu

This was actually a challenging concept for me to wrap my head around when I was first introduced to "detaching from outcome" or "letting-go" or "release." You see, I was a very Type A personality. I was a driven individual with specific and detailed goals and because of some of my past career paths, I was conditioned to believe that the outcome of the goal was all that mattered. I believed if I worked hard and never took my eye off the prize – as long I was in control, that I could achieve my goals.

But what I didn't understand was that it was the energy that I was putting into the thoughts and feelings about the goal that mattered more than the actual activity. It was my attachment to the outcome that was causing resistance. I was not living in a state of allowing – I had too many conditions about how the outcome should occur. I, in fact, was sabotaging my own success and joy. You see, in "pushing," I was pushing away my desired outcome.

One of the best resources I have found on the topic of Law of Attraction is Abraham-Hicks and I encourage you to read the books and listen to the meditation CDs and other tools they have created to help you understand the power of vibrational alignment.

"If you can reach the place where you can joyfully live with the absence of what you want to manifest because the presence of the idea of it is so delicious, then the presence of it must come to you, and will quickly."
~ Abraham-Hicks

Something I do every month on the Full Moon is a release ceremony. The full moon is the time for releasing things that no longer serve you and the new moon is about manifesting things you want. I do both moon ceremonies but I'm going to talk now about release work you can do during the full moon or really any time you want to release things, or feelings, or whatever is getting in the way of your joy.

A simple way to release thoughts and feelings you have that are getting in your way, is to blow them into a cup of water and then throw the water outside. (Don't drink it.) Water is a powerful purifier and can also be used to bathe in, especially if you bathe in salt water. It will help cleanse and purifier negative energies – another form of release. Even in the shower, as I watch the water go down the drain I motion my hands in a counter-clockwise motion to let the water take the negative energies from my mind and body.

Purifying your home is a good idea too. Diffusing sage essential oil or using a smudge stick is another great way to clear energies from your home or work space. You can go beyond that by actually "clearing" your space and your property of unwanted energies by using more advanced techniques. I won't go through these here but if you're interested in delving deeper into this subject, a great resource I've found is Christan Hummel's book, *Do-It-Yourself Space Clearing Kit* or Denise Linn's two books, *Kindling the Native Spirit* and *Energy Strands.*

If you're new to metaphysical principles, I know some of these techniques might seem a little "woo-woo" to you. But I would suggest being open; taking one step at a time and learning as much as you're comfortable with. That's what I did. There are plenty of great resources. I would suggest looking to the more well-known teachers on this subject to start with like Abraham-Hicks, Matt Kahn, Denise Linn and many others whom I have quoted in this book.

Probably the simplest way I have found to release negative thoughts so that I'm in a state of allowing is through prayer. You can do this anytime by asking the Creator or Spirit or your Angels to help you release the things you no longer wish. I actually write them down during the full moon and then either soak them in salt water or burn them after.

> ***"Prayer is not asking. It is a longing of the soul. It is daily admission of one's weakness. It is better in prayer to have a heart without words than words without a heart."***
> ~ Mahatma Gandhi

The last thing I want to share with you about the subject of release is to please release worry. It's not your responsibility to worry about something. You're not proving to others that you care more by worrying. I know many people tell me they feel guilty if they are not worrying, as if the worry has power to change the situation. As Wayne Dyer said, "You can't discover light by analyzing the darkness." So, as they say, let go and let God.

I know this is a lot of information – to some, maybe some new thoughts. For others, perhaps just a reminder to do your work. We can all get stuck in our muck from time to time and forget it was our thoughts that got us there. Time to release. Life is not a struggle. Time to allow. And that is joyful living.

Day 8

MY DAILY AFFIRMATION

Letting go is like a purge.
It cleans and clears the way
for new intentions that will serve
all those my heart does pray.

MY DAILY ACTIVITY

DECLUTTER: Make some time today to de-clutter a room or a space in your home or office. Give away or throw away items that you no longer use. Perform space clearing rituals if you wish. These acts of "release" will help to clear old energies from your home or office, making room for your new, joyful state of being.

MY DAILY FREQUENCY SHIFTER

At the end of each day, rate your state of joy on this **Joy-meter** *and then make any comments or observations about your feelings during the day or about anything noteworthy that occurred. This will help you see how your joy increases during the 40 days and what "shows up" for you.*

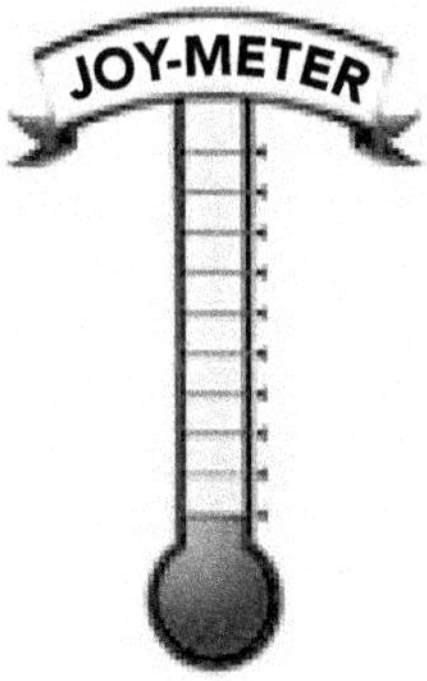

10 – Off the charts.
9 – Super amazing.
8 – Pretty blissful.
7 – Oh happy joy.
6 – I believe.
5 – I've turned the corner.
4 – I'm breathing easier.
3 – I can see the light.
2 – The clouds are lifting.
1 – I feel depressed.

NOTES

____
____
____
____
____
____
____
____
____
____
____

Day 9

BE PEACEFUL

"Lord, make me an instrument of thy peace.
Where there is hatred, let me sow love."

~Saint Francis of Assisi

"Talk peaceful to be peaceful," said Norman Vincent Peale. Don't let the simplicity of this quote slip by you. Our words and thoughts are so important. Not only to what we project outwardly, but to what we project inwardly as well. When we speak in quiet and non-aggressive tones and send out loving peaceful thoughts, we literally make change happen. Let me explain.

A few years ago, I was fortunate enough to attend a seminar lead by Dr. Masaru Emoto, a Japanese author and entrepreneur known for his research into the effect that human consciousness has on the molecular structure of water.

In his many books such as, *Messages from Water* and *Hidden Messages in Water,* which contain photographs of water crystals, Dr. Emoto claimed that high-quality water forms beautiful and intricate crystals, while low-quality water had difficulty forming crystals at all. He suggested that positive changes to water crystals could be achieved through prayer, music, or by attaching written words to a container of water.

The pictures in his books are quite amazing and I encourage you to pick up a copy of one to see for yourself. I have a poster hanging in my home of a photograph of one of the frozen crystals that has the words "thank you" written on the bottle. It is magical and beautiful – just the way loving thoughts and peace should look.

Of course, the point is that because half the earth is made of water and we are three-quarters water ourselves, what we think and say has a dramatic effect on us and on the world around us. In fact, Dr. Emoto was so inspired by his findings that in May 2005 he launched the Emoto Peace Project, which aims at teaching the truth about water to children throughout the world.

In a quote from the Emoto Peace Project website, Dr. Emoto says: "We have learned that our human consciousness is related to water at deeper level through water crystal technology. And this fact has resonated with different people in different countries. However, this fact has not been taught at any school. The words "Thank you" have positive vibrations and the words "You fool" have negative vibrations and to ignore is to deny the existence itself and this will give the most negative effects."

In this day and age when school bullying and violence is commonplace, I believe that work like that of Dr. Emoto is profoundly important. I believe we all want more peace in our world, in our countries, in our cities, in our homes, and in our hearts. But that starts with us. As Robert Fulghum said: "Peace is not something you wish for. It's something you make, something you do, something you are, and something you give away."

"Peace is a higher and faster energy – when you're being peace, just your presence alone will often nullify the uneasiness or tension in those around you. In fact, this state causes pheromones of measurable energy to emanate from you.
They affect others, who become more peaceful without even being aware of the transformation taking place."
~ Wayne Dyer – *Being in Balance*

Please pray for your own peace of mind and for that of others. And then listen. Remember, when you pray, you are talking to God. When you are at peace and in meditation, that's when God talks to you. And that is joyful living.

Day 9

MY DAILY AFFIRMATION

I speak to myself with love today.
My words are gentle and kind.
I am at peace.
I've been released.
My heart is now leading my mind.

MY DAILY ACTIVITY

MEDITATE: Make time today for a fifteen-minute meditation. If you already meditate, then add this special session with the intention of just being at peace. If you haven't meditated before, then set a timer for fifteen minutes and sit quietly with legs and arms unfolded and eyes closed, and focus on your breathing and the peace you feel as you relax into your heart and your breath. Just a short fifteen-minute meditation each day can do wonders for stress-relief and move you closer to a life of peace and joy.

MY DAILY FREQUENCY SHIFTER

At the end of each day, rate your state of joy on this **Joy-meter** *and then make any comments or observations about your feelings during the day or about anything noteworthy that occurred. This will help you see how your joy increases during the 40 days and what "shows up" for you.*

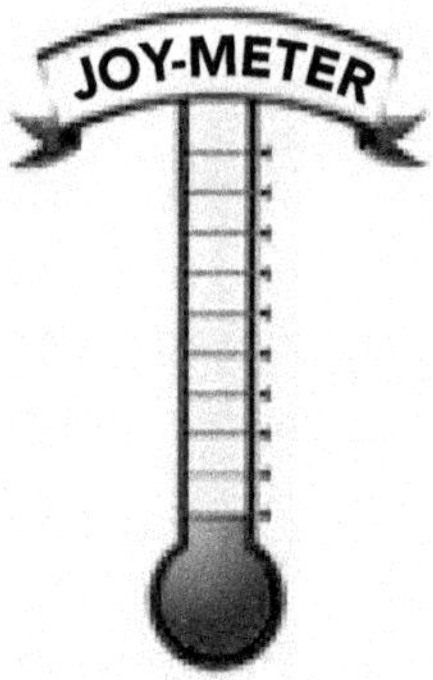

10 – Off the charts.
9 – Super amazing.
8 – Pretty blissful.
7 – Oh happy joy.
6 – I believe.
5 – I've turned the corner.
4 – I'm breathing easier.
3 – I can see the light.
2 – The clouds are lifting.
1 – I feel depressed.

NOTES

Day 9

MORE NOTES

Day 10

BE PRESENT

"I am in the right place, at the right time,
doing the right thing."

~ Louise L Hay

We are all so busy these days. We exist under this great delusion of urgency. Rushing here and rushing there. Kids to pick up. Deadlines to meet. And your to-do list just keeps getting longer. But here's the deal. You're never going to get it all done. You're not actually supposed to. Shocking, isn't it? This is what I mean.

I believe the whole point of living your most amazing life is to take it all in. Enjoy your busy-ness as that's propelling you forward. But know that as soon as you tick something off the list, you are going to replace it with something else. That's life. It's never going to get all done. And that's o.k. So, give yourself a break.

You see, I believe that the energy you put into every task, whether it is driving to work, preparing a meal, or doing the laundry has value and should be honoured. Try to be mindful with each activity. Resist the compulsion to multi-task. For it's in moments of each activity where you actually live. It's where you are right now. There is no past and no future. Just now. So, enjoy it.

"You cannot be both unhappy and fully present in the Now."

~ Eckhart Tolle

So, let's dive a little deeper. The practice of present-moment mindfulness is one that can bring you great clarity, peace, and the fastest way to joy. It's about the three A's:

Awareness

Appreciation

Acceptance

It's a practice of reprogramming yourself so that you value all moments, without judgement. It's so you can live more in a state of "being-ness" rather than in the expectation of fulfilled desires. Living in the now. Believe me, once you start to do this, you'll feel an energy shift in yourself – an elevated frequency that will help you feel a greater sense of peace and joy.

> ***"The time to blossom is now, not sometime in the future when you believe the stars will be aligned for you."***
> ~ Madisyn Taylor

Now let's move a little deeper still.

One of the leading authorities on the power of present-moment living and the importance of stillness is Eckhart Tolle. One of my favourite books of his is called, *Stillness Speaks.* It makes a lovely gift book, so I would suggest you buy one for yourself and one to give to someone you care about. (That's what I usually do.)

I think a great way to start your practice of mindfulness is to practice stillness first. In his book, Tolle begins by saying, "When you lose touch with inner stillness, you lose touch with yourself. When you lose touch with yourself, you lose yourself in the world. Your innermost sense of self, of who you are, is inseparable from stillness. This is the I AM that is deeper than name and form."

"Adopt the pace of nature: her secret is patience."

~ Ralph Waldo Emerson

Tolle, as well as many other thought-leaders, poets, and spiritual teachers talks about the significant role that nature plays for healing our physical, emotional and spiritual needs as we move through every stage of our lives.

I know for myself, just sitting beneath a tree or walking through a forest in silent reflection, can soothe me like nothing else. If you can, try to get outdoors at least once a day and commune with nature. It can be as simple as walking to the park and sitting on the bench. Better still, walk barefoot on the grass during the summer and feel Mother Nature's energy pulsating through your veins. Feel the stillness. Be present. Look inside. That's where the peace lives. And that is joyful living.

Day 10

MY DAILY AFFIRMATION

I breathe in. I breathe out.
In this stillness I see
that to live in the moment
is to honour the "me."

MY DAILY ACTIVITY

COMMUNE WITH NATURE: If the weather permits, take a twenty to thirty-minute walk where there are trees or other forms of nature. If that's not possible, go to a flower shop or garden centre and breathe in the scent of nature. Diffuse high-quality, grounding essential oils like cedarwood, spruce, cypress, or balsam fir and breathe deeply while you commune with nature. Be still. Be quiet. There is nowhere else for you to be but here… now. Breathe, be present, and feel the joy.

MY DAILY FREQUENCY SHIFTER

At the end of each day, rate your state of joy on this **Joy-meter** *and then make any comments or observations about your feelings during the day or about anything noteworthy that occurred. This will help you see how your joy increases during the 40 days and what "shows up" for you.*

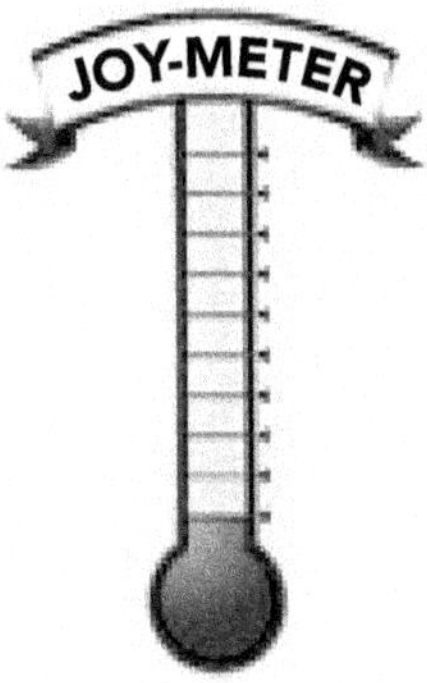

10 – Off the charts.
9 – Super amazing.
8 – Pretty blissful.
7 – Oh happy joy.
6 – I believe.
5 – I've turned the corner.
4 – I'm breathing easier.
3 – I can see the light.
2 – The clouds are lifting.
1 – I feel depressed.

NOTES

Day 10

Day 11

BE GRATEFUL

"Joy is what happens to us when we allow ourselves to recognize how good things really are."

~ Marianne Williamson

Buddhists say to be a good fisherman, you much detach yourself from the dream of the fish. That makes whatever is caught or found a treasure.

The subject of gratitude has been rich with wisdom from many great thinkers over the years. It's such a universal understanding – that to receive further abundance in life, you must first give thanks for what you have.

However, I believe that gratitude and appreciation are a bit different from each other. In my mind, appreciation is the action of expressing thanks for or because of something that happens; whereas gratitude is a state of being. For example, having a grateful heart would mean living in a state where you appreciate everything that comes your way, because after-all, you actually intended it.

I know for a fact that by living with a grateful heart you will be happier, less stressed, and attract more abundance and joy into your life than you will by complaining about what you don't have. There is an Estonian proverb that goes – "Who does not thank for little will not thank for much." You see, it's simply the Law of Attraction at work. And it always works.

Most of us have heard about the benefits of writing in a gratitude journal every day. Or before going to bed, recalling three things that you are grateful for. Once you have retrained your brain to think in "asset" terms instead of "deficit" terms – focusing on what you have instead of what you don't, gratitude thinking will become a new pattern of being for you.

"What a wonderful life I've had.
I only wish I'd realized it sooner."
~ Colette

Once you adjust your mind-set, you'll become more aligned with the high vibration of joy, where your state of allowing will bring many blessings into your life. You will achieve a greater sense of wonder about life – seeing everything as valuable and with meaning. And when you regularly give thanks, even more magic will befall you.

"Be grateful for whoever comes, because each has been sent as a guide from beyond."
~Rumi

So, my beloved reader, if you are currently struggling with a challenge and are feeling a "lack" in your life, adopt a new attitude for gratitude. Pause and look for the learning in that situation – usually the best gifts come from overcoming a challenge or obstacle you are facing. And if you're looking for more inspiration about how gratitude can be a powerful force for living a more joyful life, I suggest visiting this amazing website and movement founded by Brother David Steindl-Rast at www.gratefullness.org.

I'll close this chapter with another proverb that I hope will inspire your heart, a French one this time. "Gratitude is the heart's memory." How simple. How true. And that indeed is joyful living.

Day 11

MY DAILY AFFIRMATION

My gifts are rich with meaning.
They always have a plan.
Although I may not see them,
my spirit always can.

MY DAILY ACTIVITY

GRATITUDE JOURNAL: I've found writing in my Gratitude Journal each morning is a fantastic way to elevate my joyful frequency for the day. Find a nice book that you like and a nice pen to write with. I write down ten things I'm thankful for each day. They can be as simple as what I ate for breakfast, if it was really yummy, to people I am grateful for, or things that happened yesterday or I'm intending to happen today, or the way I'm feeling. The important thing is to do it every day – make it a habit. You'll notice that you start to attract far more blessings into your life by having a grateful heart.

MY DAILY FREQUENCY SHIFTER

At the end of each day, rate your state of joy on this **Joy-meter** *and then make any comments or observations about your feelings during the day or about anything noteworthy that occurred. This will help you see how your joy increases during the 40 days and what "shows up" for you.*

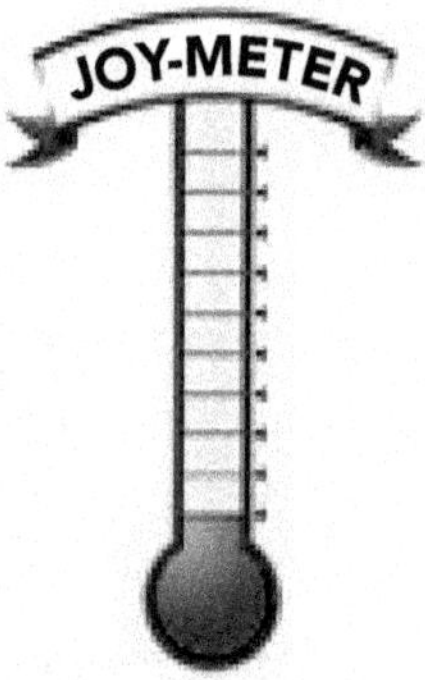

10 – Off the charts.
9 – Super amazing.
8 – Pretty blissful.
7 – Oh happy joy.
6 – I believe.
5 – I've turned the corner.
4 – I'm breathing easier.
3 – I can see the light.
2 – The clouds are lifting.
1 – I feel depressed.

NOTES

Day 11

MORE NOTES

Day 12

BE RENEWED

"Every morning we are born again.
What we do today is what matters most."

~Buddha

One of the things I most enjoy about New Year's Day is my annual ritual of reflection on the past year's learning and redefining my intentions for the year ahead. I'm not a huge fan of New Year's resolutions as I find they can be too self-punishing if you don't keep one. I prefer to look at the year as a time of renewal – like having a giant "do-over" for the next twelve months. That's something I can get excited about.

I set the big intentions, keeping in mind not to get in my own way by putting all the "hows" into the equation. I just set the big stuff and do my best to let my inner guidance direct the course I'm to take for the next months.

But you don't have to wait until January 1st to do this. Every day is actually a do-over. Every morning you can look at what happened the day before and decide what will best guide you for today. Then set your intentions for the day at hand and be joyful as you do it.

"The flower that wilted last year is gone. Petals once fallen are fallen forever. Flowers do not return in the spring, rather they are replaced. It is in this difference between returned and replaced that the price of renewal is paid. And as it is for spring flowers, so it is for us."

~ Daniel Abraham, *The Price of Spring*

Renewal is taking a big exhale and saying – "Today's a new day. I get to co-create it the way I want by the way I think and feel. I am grateful for yesterday's teachings, but they no longer exist except in my memory if I choose to recall them. They have served their purpose and now is now. Today I begin anew."

This is such an empowering exercise. It releases you from any baggage you might be carrying over from yesterday and opens the door for you to forgive yourself and others. It's a clean slate. Time to get on with it.

"Things are always better in the morning."
~ Harper Lee, *To Kill a Mockingbird*

I've found that many people spend more time living in the past than they do in this very moment – in this new day of possibility. And when you do that, as we learned in Chapter 10 about Being Present, living in the past, kicking yourself for what you believe you should of, would of, could of, simply focuses your attention on what you don't want instead of what you do. And that's the fastest way to stop the flow of abundance and joy from showing up in your life.

Remember, you are the co-creator of your own experiences – don't give away your power to the past. Shed the old and renew yourself each day. Define who you want to be today. It really is that simple. And that is joyful living.

Day 12

MY DAILY AFFIRMATION

I choose today to be reborn.
To start this day anew.
To rid myself of worry and fear.
To let my light shine through.

MY DAILY ACTIVITY

FAN LETTER: Write a fan letter to yourself and mail it. What a lift it will be when you open the letter you wrote describing the "new joyful you" and what you admire about the new you. Get mushy. Really write like an admiring fan. Then feel renewed as you begin to live the joyful life you've imagined.

MY DAILY FREQUENCY SHIFTER

At the end of each day, rate your state of joy on this **Joy-meter** *and then make any comments or observations about your feelings during the day or about anything noteworthy that occurred. This will help you see how your joy increases during the 40 days and what "shows up" for you.*

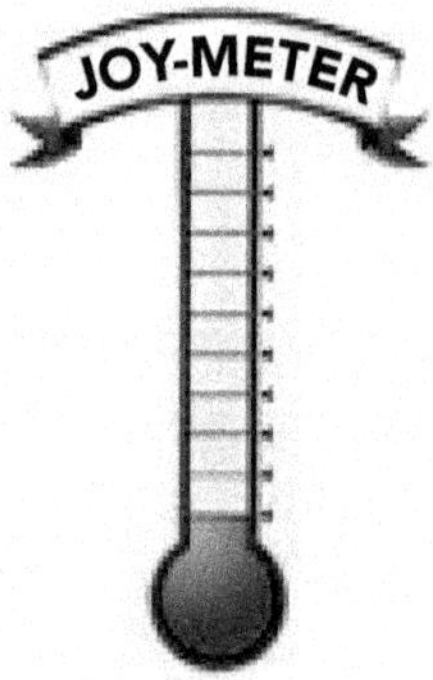

10 – Off the charts.
9 – Super amazing.
8 – Pretty blissful.
7 – Oh happy joy.
6 – I believe.
5 – I've turned the corner.
4 – I'm breathing easier.
3 – I can see the light.
2 – The clouds are lifting.
1 – I feel depressed.

NOTES

___

___

___

___

___

___

___

___

___

___

___

Day 12

MORE NOTES

Day 13

BE FLEXIBLE

"Steadiness is essential
Forwards or backwards
Let us not look.
Let us learn to live swaying
As a rocking boat on the sea."

~ Friedrich Hölderlin

Jason Kravitz said, "Be infinitely flexible and constantly amazed." Love that one. It reminds me of the importance of being open. Flexibility and openness to me are one and the same. And out of openness come experiences and opportunities that can't even be imagined. So, get ready to be amazed.

But how to be flexible when so many people around you can appear to be so rigid, want their own way, or are not prepared to compromise? How can you remain flexible and open without feeling like you're giving in? It's not an easy thing but with a loving heart and some help, it can turn into a new way of being.

Stephen R. Covey talks about this is his classic bestseller, *The 7 Habits of Highly Effective People*. In Covey's Habit #4, Think Win-Win, Covey explains that "Think Win-Win isn't about being nice, nor is it a quick-fix technique. It is a character-based code for human interaction and collaboration."

He continues to say that so many of us have been conditioned to value or in most cases de-value our worth by comparing ourselves to others. Often, we believe there isn't enough to go around – that if you win, that means I lose or if I win, you lose.

When people are fearful of change, they can retreat into seeing themselves as victims, having given away their power, believing that's just the way it is. All this rigid and uncompromising thinking does is create competitiveness instead of collaboration and hostility rather than peace. And in this scenario, does anyone really win? And in fact, should that really be the objective?

"The measure of intelligence is the ability to change."
~ Albert Einstein

When our intention is win-win, we are operating from our highest selves. Our goal then is to achieve an outcome that's good for all parties because we believe there's enough for everyone. We think in terms of "and" instead of "either/or."

But learning to be more flexible requires personal change. It's about balancing consideration and empathy for others with confidence in your own values and points of view. It's about being vulnerable.

A terrific book that I highly recommend is *Daring Greatly* by Brené Brown. This is such a powerful read about how to transform the way you live your life through the grace of vulnerability.

By being flexible, you look at each interaction you have with others as an opportunity to practice your win-win mindset with the understanding that being flexible is a sign of wisdom and strength and not of weakness.

"The best chance to be whole is to love whatever gets in the way until it ceases to be an obstacle."
~Mark Nepo

Flexibility is also about learning to be more open to your own expectations of what you think you should be or do or have. Time to exhale here. You've been holding your breath far too long trying to be perfect.

You see, we can sometimes get rigid about what we think should happen in our lives. In fact, by being rigid we stop the flow of opportunities. We apply too much effort to our thoughts. (And effort kills flow.) How can you follow the course of your life if you do not let it flow?

Like martial arts superstar Bruce Lee said, "Empty your mind, be formless, shapeless – like water. Now you put water into a cup, it becomes the cup, you put water into a bottle, it becomes the bottle, you put it in a teapot, it becomes the teapot. Now water can flow, or it can crash. Be water, my friend."

So today I challenge you to be more open and flexible in all your thoughts and deeds and as Bruce Lee said, "Be water, my friend." And that is joyful living.

Day 13

MY DAILY AFFIRMATION

I sway with the wind.
I bend now with ease.
I see spirit in others.
We just all want to be.

MY DAILY ACTIVITY

STRETCH & SWAY: A simple activity today, but an important one for helping move energy through your body with ease. Spend a few minutes today stretching your entire body as far as you can. Then sway back and forth, in a slow and easy motion. Make each movement gentle and mindful. If you can, sway to some peaceful music or hum. And remember that as your body learns to be flexible, you will learn inside as well. Stretch and sway, stretch and sway, stretch and sway...

MY DAILY FREQUENCY SHIFTER

At the end of each day, rate your state of joy on this **Joy-meter** *and then make any comments or observations about your feelings during the day or about anything noteworthy that occurred. This will help you see how your joy increases during the 40 days and what "shows up" for you.*

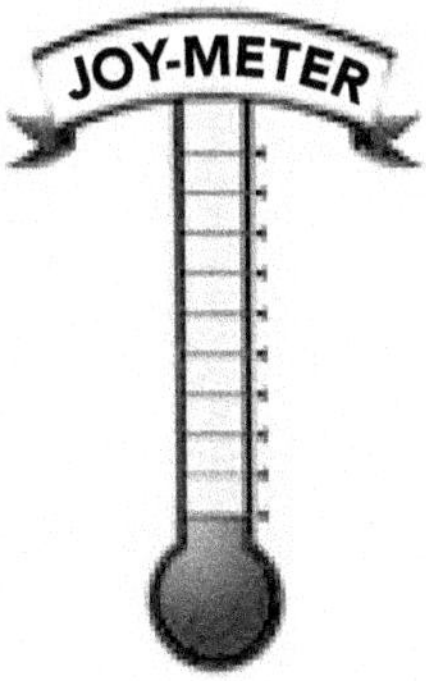

10 – Off the charts.
9 – Super amazing.
8 – Pretty blissful.
7 – Oh happy joy.
6 – I believe.
5 – I've turned the corner.
4 – I'm breathing easier.
3 – I can see the light.
2 – The clouds are lifting.
1 – I feel depressed.

NOTES

Day 13

Day 14

BE RELAXED

"One of the symptoms of an approaching nervous breakdown is the belief that one's work is terribly important."

~ Bertrand Russell

I really chuckled when I first read that quote by Bertrand Russell on the cover page to this chapter. We sure can take ourselves seriously, can't we? That's just another way for the ego to manifest itself into stress and worry, depleting our energy and lowering our frequency.

So, with that said, today's topic may be a challenge for some of you. For people who are used to "go-go-go," in particular, working moms, the thought of trying to carve out a few minutes of "me-time" each day can be stressful in itself. You immediately go to, *What won't get done if I take some time for myself?*

But I ask you instead, what is the real cost to your life of not learning to prioritize some personal time each day, just for you? Not only are you devaluing your own worth, but you are teaching others – your children, your partner, your co-workers, that you aren't important. But you are.

You see, relaxation, whether it be by taking a hot bubble bath, or reading a book, or going on a nature walk, is not only good for the body, it is essential for the spirit. Here's what I mean.

"The time to relax is when you don't have time for it."
~Attributed to both Jim Goodwin and Sydney J. Harris

You probably already know that stress can seriously increase your risk of high blood pressure, heart attack, and other heart problems. Other studies have found that stress increases the amount of some proteins in the brain that have already been linked to Alzheimer's disease. There is also some evidence linking stress with some types of cancer.

Not only that, when you are living with constant stress, you elevate the presence of the stress hormone cortisol, which interferes with your body's ability to produce serotonin and dopamine. That can lead to depression. And when you are depressed, you can't feel joyful.

When you don't allow yourself time to unwind, you are actually living in chronic stress. Research tells us that stress can kill brain cells and even prevent the creation of new ones.

"Work is not always required. There is such a thing as sacred idleness."
~George MacDonald

Ok, are you convinced yet that stress reduction is essential for living a balanced life of joy? In fact, as women's health expert Dr. Christine Northrup says – "Joy increases the level of DHEA life force, which affects hormone levels." By relaxing more and stressing less, you'll live more joyfully. So, in fact, joy can help you live longer.

Now, let's see what else relaxation can do for you.

"Most rarely align with their true power, because it seems illogical to them that there is power in relaxation, in letting go, or in love or joy or bliss. Most people do not understand that their true power lies in releasing resistance – which is the only obstacle to their true power."
~ Abraham-Hicks

Well for starters, when you're not stressed, you have better clarity of thought. You make better decisions. When you're not stressed, you're generally not focused on problems, you're more positive, your vibrational frequency is higher, and you feel like you're operating on all cylinders.

When you're not stressed, you generally have a healthier diet. You've likely heard or said to yourself while reaching for a big bowl of ice-cream or potato chips that, "I'm just eating my feelings." And we all know where that leads.

Relaxation also helps with the health of your complexion and the clearness in your eyes. When you're relaxed, your body is healthier, and it will show. Also, you will likely find an improvement in your libido.

So please, make a commitment to yourself today to relax more and work less, to love more and compare less, and to allow more and resist less. And that is joyful living.

Day 14

MY DAILY AFFIRMATION

I give myself the gift of rest
although my list's not done.
I exhale all the weight & pressure
and inhale all the fun.

MY DAILY ACTIVITY

MINDFUL BREATHING: As you move through your day, be mindful of your breathing. Is it slow and peaceful or do you hold your breath when upset? Breathe from your belly as in Dr. Andrew Weil's techniques for breathing, one of which is as follows:

"Exhale completely through your mouth, making a whoosh sound.

Close your mouth and inhale quietly through your nose to a mental count of **four**.

Hold your breath for a count of **seven**.

Exhale completely through your mouth, making a whoosh sound to a count of **eight**.

This is one breath. Now inhale again and repeat the cycle three more times for a total of four breaths."

MY DAILY FREQUENCY SHIFTER

At the end of each day, rate your state of joy on this **Joy-meter** *and then make any comments or observations about your feelings during the day or about anything noteworthy that occurred. This will help you see how your joy increases during the 40 days and what "shows up" for you.*

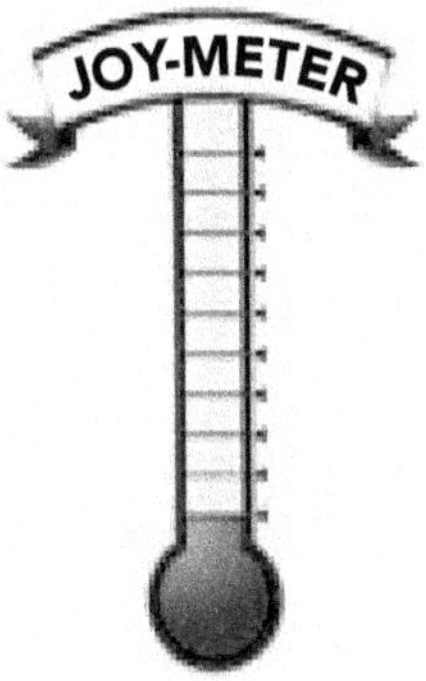

10 – Off the charts.
9 – Super amazing.
8 – Pretty blissful.
7 – Oh happy joy.
6 – I believe.
5 – I've turned the corner.
4 – I'm breathing easier.
3 – I can see the light.
2 – The clouds are lifting.
1 – I feel depressed.

NOTES

Day 14

Day 15

BE ACCEPTING

"The fact that you are willing to say,
'I do not understand, and it is fine,'
is the greatest understanding you could exhibit."

~ Wayne Dyer

"Life doesn't happen to me. Life happens for me."

I'm not sure who said this quote first, but I heard Deepak Chopra say it on a CD I have, and I've found it to be one of the more impactful quotes I've heard. Certainly, it makes the case for not living as a victim. This is what I mean.

We're all bound to have things happen that we don't expect or even understand for that matter. You're running late and get a parking ticket. You lock yourself out of your house. You spill coffee on a clean shirt. Your company is downsizing, and you've been laid off. At times like this, it's easy to say, "Why me?" and to feel like a victim.

But when we pause and accept there are no accidents, that everything that happens has meaning and purpose, then we can grow. In fact, as Denise Linn says, "Acceptance is a sacred act of power." I agree.

"Accepting means you allow yourself to feel whatever it is you are feeling at that moment. It is part of the isness of the Now. You can't argue with what is. Well, you can, but if you do, you suffer."

~Eckhart Tolle

Think about an event that has happened to you recently when you felt like a victim – maybe it was even today. Most of us face life's little disturbances several times a day. Some big – some small. These are just opportunities for learning and growth; as challenging as they may feel at the time.

The important thing to ask when they happen is not "Why me?" or "Why did this happen?" but "What is this trying to show me or teach me?" and "What can I take away from this situation to help me with the next challenge?" That's how we all learn; by making mistakes, by having "accidents," and by colliding with the world around us. Life happens. It's what we learn from the experience that will determine how we react to the next one. Ask the "What" not the "Why."

Not only will surrendering to the moment enable you to have less anxiety about the situation but once you start to accept more, you'll begin to understand that often a course change brings you to your desired outcome faster and better.

Let's use an example to illustrate the relevance of this topic throughout this joy journey you are on. Let's say you've set a goal of getting a promotion at your workplace. You're been there a while and feel you deserve it. You would really like to take a big vacation next year to see family you haven't seen in a while and the promotion would give you a bigger salary, along with a larger office and more responsibility.

You are very single-minded about this. To you, there are no other options. You just want that promotion. Even though you really don't like the company you work for, the extra money will make it all worth it.

But because you are so rigid about seeing only one solution for taking that dream vacation, you dismiss the "chance" meeting with an old friend who offers to introduce you to the HR person at her company. It's in the industry that appeals to you more than where you are, but because you are reluctant to change, you say thanks but no thanks.

You don't get the promotion you want, but you do get a bit more money. However, now you have a lot more responsibility and are working longer hours doing a job you really don't like. And once vacation time comes along, you are too busy to take your trip back home to visit your loved ones. And now you hear rumours that the company is down-sizing.

Your inability to let go of your single-minded desperation for more money to travel home didn't allow you to see any other solutions. To make matters worse, you later learn that the company your friend suggested has a branch office closer to where your family lives.

"The ultimate act of power is surrender."
~ Krishna Das

You see, the Universe sees the big picture. It's heard you and always provides various courses for you to take. But because we have free will, we get to choose which path to take. And more often than not, we will experience plenty of detours along the way to our desired destination. So, my point here is to allow, allow, allow. Like you learned in Chapter 13, let go of your anxiety and don't let your inflexibility block the flow of other opportunities from coming into your life. Expand your perspective through acceptance of where you are right now.

Remember, acceptance is not giving in. And surrender is not giving up. It's about letting go of your need to control. Letting go of the ego.

Acceptance is a state of consciousness that honours the events of your life as a teaching experience. It provides you with confidence in a Universe that is conspiring on your behalf and always providing opportunities for your personal growth. And in practicing acceptance you gain wisdom and a greater peace of mind without the compulsion to control.

So, the next time something happens that you haven't expected or can't explain or understand, don't get frustrated or curse the situation. Don't look for people or things to blame. Let go. Thank the experience. It is your gift of growth along the path you have chosen. And that is joyful living.

Day 15

MY DAILY AFFIRMATION

I trust that Spirit has a plan
that serves my highest good.
I'm not a victim nor am I weak.
I surrender as I should.

MY DAILY ACTIVITY

LET GO: Make a list of the three areas of your life where you try to control other people or situations. Awareness is the first step. Now list things you could do to begin to let go. Surrender is a process. Be patient with yourself.

MY DAILY FREQUENCY SHIFTER

At the end of each day, rate your state of joy on this **Joy-meter** *and then make any comments or observations about your feelings during the day or about anything noteworthy that occurred. This will help you see how your joy increases during the 40 days and what "shows up" for you.*

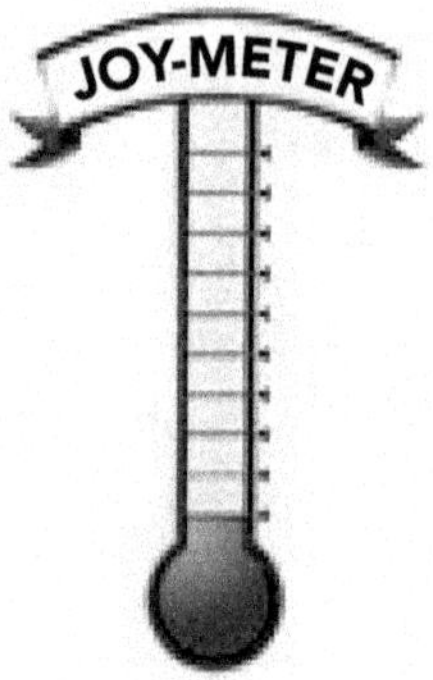

10 – Off the charts.
9 – Super amazing.
8 – Pretty blissful.
7 – Oh happy joy.
6 – I believe.
5 – I've turned the corner.
4 – I'm breathing easier.
3 – I can see the light.
2 – The clouds are lifting.
1 – I feel depressed.

NOTES

Day 15

MORE NOTES

Day 16

BE CREATIVE

"Working hard for something we don't care about
is called stress;
working hard for something we love
is called passion."

~ Simon Sinek

Creativity. One of my favourite topics. Ever since I can remember, I was drawn to creative pursuits. And I've always known I was a rebel.

I started writing poetry at age thirteen when my dad brought home a tiny yellow rhyming dictionary from one of his business trips, (which I am proud to say I still have and use to this day).

I would write plays with my friends as well as short stories and outlines for novels. I wanted to be a writer. I was going to go to university to get my journalism degree after graduation. But it was the early seventies and I got distracted and never went. I continued to write anyway for fun and then commercially as a way to earn a living. Just because I didn't have a degree didn't mean I couldn't write. The rebel in me would not be silenced.

Others find their creative passion through visual arts. My son is a talented painter. He paints houses for a living, but in his spare time he can be found at home working on large pieces of canvas, expressing his inner feelings with acrylics or stencilling on fabric. He's also a rebel.

"Passion is the currency of co-creation."
~ Anonymous

I know people who love to sing and dance. They are truly in their joy as they move their bodies or raise their voices in creative expression. Others find their creative passion in the kitchen preparing yummy treats to share with friends and family. All rebels in my opinion.

You see, to me, being creative is like being a rebel. You want to change something through your own unique expression. And if it is wrong, well so be it. After all, there really isn't any such thing as wrong anyway – there's just different.

"To live a creative life, we must lose our fear of being wrong."
~ Joseph Chilton Pearce

Rebels aren't afraid of being different. They know they are and they embrace it. Their creative energy fuels everything they do and how they think. Their imagination is what brings about innovation in our world. Bravo for the rebels among us.

So today, look deep inside for your own rebel. It will be there to some degree. You see, we all have creative energy – it's really our life force at work to make our time here more interesting and enables us to serve the world and improve the human condition.

Just go ahead and imagine it. Then use it. We'll all be better off because you did. And that is joyful living.

Day 16

MY DAILY AFFIRMATION

I show my true self
through expression today.
I am fearless and happy
as my heart leads the way.

MY DAILY ACTIVITY

LET YOUR CREATIVE BEING SHINE: Make a few minutes today to ignite your inner rebel through creative expression. Write, draw, paint, colour, sing, dance, sew, or do anything that provides the creative outlet your heart has been aching for.

MY DAILY FREQUENCY SHIFTER

At the end of each day, rate your state of joy on this **Joy-meter** *and then make any comments or observations about your feelings during the day or about anything noteworthy that occurred. This will help you see how your joy increases during the 40 days and what "shows up" for you.*

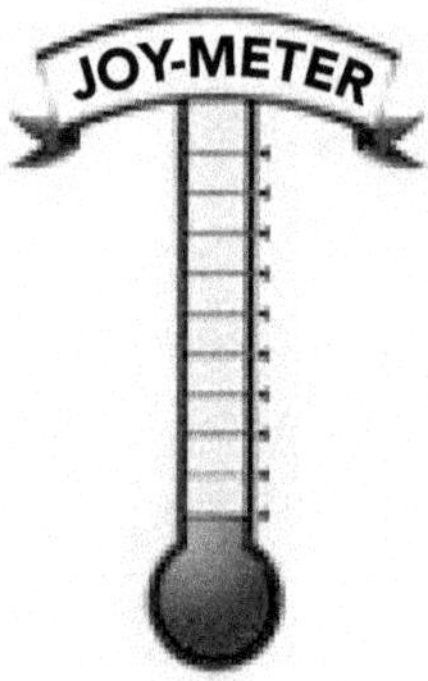

10 – Off the charts.
9 – Super amazing.
8 – Pretty blissful.
7 – Oh happy joy.
6 – I believe.
5 – I've turned the corner.
4 – I'm breathing easier.
3 – I can see the light.
2 – The clouds are lifting.
1 – I feel depressed.

NOTES

Day 16

MORE NOTES

Day 17

BE ACCOUNTABLE

"Seek not to be admired but believed."

~ Tudor Vianu

I believe that being accountable is about more than being reliable. Yes, on the surface being reliable is important. It creates a bond of trust between you and others because they know you will follow through – that you're good for your word.

However, if your agreement or promise isn't coming from an authentic place, then it's really not you who is showing up for someone else. This is what I mean.

I find that many people are often more preoccupied with having the respect of other people than respect for themselves. And when that happens, you find yourself agreeing to do something that you really don't want to do or feel comfortable with. At that point you are going against your authentic self, the one who knows what's in your best interest. And you'll likely feel it in your body – usually in your gut.

"When we fail to set boundaries and hold people accountable, we feel used and mistreated. This is why we sometimes attack who they are, which is far more hurtful than addressing a behavior or a choice."

~ Brené Brown

Refrain from saying "yes" to everyone's requests just to be nice or to have their favour or because it's easier. In the end, you'll feel resentful and won't be living in integrity with yourself.

Accountability starts with self, knowing that you are the co-creator of all your own experiences and that includes what you agree to or promise yourself and what you don't.

Take for example making New Year's resolutions. Perhaps you've fallen into the trap of making a long list of resolutions on January 1st. But by about February or March, you find it challenging to sustain your resolutions and wonder why you came up with them in the first place.

Perhaps you made that resolution because of someone else – to please them, but in your mind, you really didn't want to change that behaviour or even believe you could. Belief is such a key factor for change. You must believe in it and in yourself to make it stick. So, then you feel bad about yourself. You feel like a failure because you couldn't keep your resolution. The problem isn't your lack of willpower. It's that you didn't really believe it in the first place – you just pretended. Can't be authentic when you pretend.

"You may believe that you are responsible for what you do but not what you think. The truth is that you are responsible for what you think because it is only at this level that you can exercise this choice. What you do comes from what you think."
~ Marianne Williamson

Accountability and authenticity are inextricably linked. For when you are truly accountable to yourself, taking complete responsibility for everything that shows up in your life without judgement, you are revealing your true essence. It's how you see yourself and how you will reveal yourself to others. And that is joyful living.

Day 17

MY DAILY AFFIRMATION

Being true to myself
Is all I can be.
With my word as my honour
they'll see the real me.

MY DAILY ACTIVITY

PROMISES: Make one new promise to yourself or others that you believe can be sustained over the next 40 days. It can be big or small, but please make it something new – that you're not already doing – something you want to change or improve on. The important thing is that you are doing this because it will come from your authentic self and that you are going to hold yourself accountable for keeping the promise. At the end of 40 days, do something special to honour your kept commitment.

MY DAILY FREQUENCY SHIFTER

At the end of each day, rate your state of joy on this **Joy-meter** *and then make any comments or observations about your feelings during the day or about anything noteworthy that occurred. This will help you see how your joy increases during the 40 days and what "shows up" for you.*

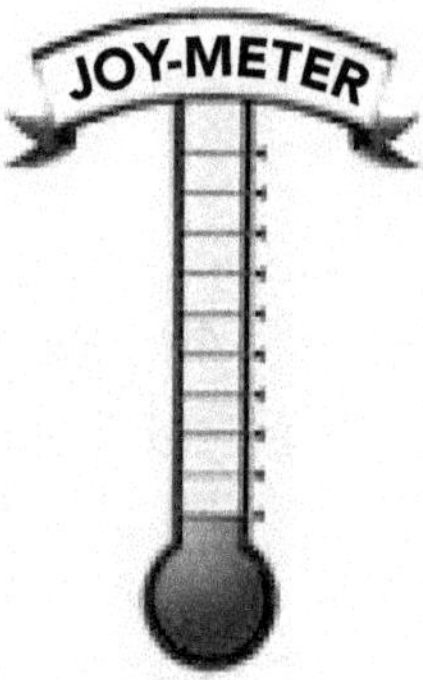

10 – Off the charts.
9 – Super amazing.
8 – Pretty blissful.
7 – Oh happy joy.
6 – I believe.
5 – I've turned the corner.
4 – I'm breathing easier.
3 – I can see the light.
2 – The clouds are lifting.
1 – I feel depressed.

NOTES

Day 17

MORE NOTES

Day 18

BE SATISFIED

"Strive for excellence, not perfection."

~ H. Jackson Brown Jr.

Are you a perfectionist? Do you feel anxious if your to-do list isn't done at the end of every day? Do you like things to be done a certain way – every time? Well maybe just a little?

You're not alone. And believe me this can be a real joy sucker.

Why do we place such high expectations on ourselves? I know many of us have been hard-wired since birth to be competitive, to judge our own value by how we compare ourselves to others. We have been conditioned to believe that perfection is the standard that we should strive for. No wonder we have so many people of all ages feeling anxious and unworthy.

As our lives continue to feel busier than ever before, it's difficult to balance your belief that things must be perfect with the feeling that time is just moving too quickly to get it all done.

"Striving for excellence motivates you; striving for perfection is demoralizing."

~ Harriet Braiker

I know this only too well, because for many years I joked that I had two speeds – warp speed and stop. There simply wasn't anything in-between. I was fueled by the misconception that being perfect at running my companies and raising a child on my own, made me a better person. All this did was put me on a collision course with emotional, physical, and spiritual illness.

Once I realized that perfection really shouldn't be the goal, I started to ease up on myself. But it was a process. Being a Type A personality who has always been driven to create new things and explore uncharted territory in record time meant that I needed to learn a new operating system for life. And it started by being kinder to myself.

> ***"It is better to live your own destiny imperfectly than to live an imitation of somebody else's life with perfection."***
> ~The Bhagavad Gita

If this sounds familiar to you, then you'll want to stop believing that everything has to be perfect, and that you have to be perfect. It won't be, and you can't be. Because in that struggle for perfection, you beat yourself up and feel inadequate for not measuring up. And that only attracts more negative feelings and more negative self-talk.

So what if the tablecloth doesn't fit perfectly. No problem that you didn't get the car washed today. Don't sweat it if your favourite serving platter has a crack in it. After all, as the late Leonard Cohen said it, "There's a crack in everything. That's how the light gets in." Love him and miss his poetic voice.

Give yourself a break. You did your best. Time to let the light in. For as you look at your list of tasks undone by day's end, remind yourself that good enough is good enough. And that is joyful living.

Day 18

MY DAILY AFFIRMATION

Joy & contentment
come easily to me
when I stop seeing perfect
as the only way to be.

MY DAILY ACTIVITY

DON'T SWEAT THE SMALL STUFF: Make a point of catching yourself when you feel critical of yourself or others today. Instead, breathe and relax into the contentment of accepting yourself and others just the way you are. Be mindful of the temptation to fuss or tidy things – just for one day. And repeat the mantra, "Good enough is good enough." You can do it.

MY DAILY FREQUENCY SHIFTER

At the end of each day, rate your state of joy on this **Joy-meter** *and then make any comments or observations about your feelings during the day or about anything noteworthy that occurred. This will help you see how your joy increases during the 40 days and what "shows up" for you.*

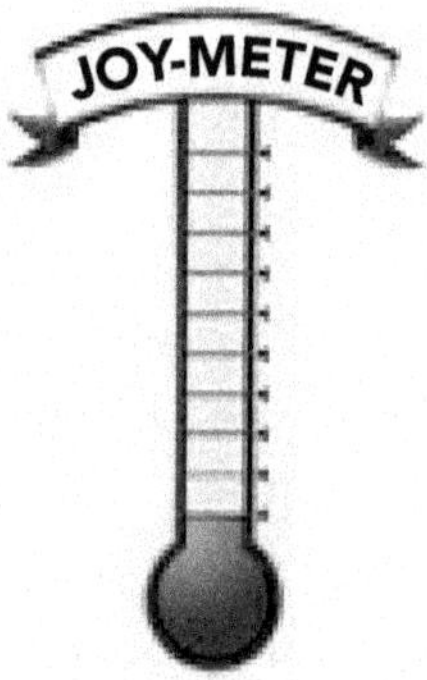

10 – Off the charts.
9 – Super amazing.
8 – Pretty blissful.
7 – Oh happy joy.
6 – I believe.
5 – I've turned the corner.
4 – I'm breathing easier.
3 – I can see the light.
2 – The clouds are lifting.
1 – I feel depressed.

NOTES

___
___
___
___
___
___
___
___
___
___
___

Day 18

MORE NOTES

Day 19

BE IN SPIRIT

"If we do not know what port we're steering for, no wind is favorable."

~Seneca

Today's subject is about being more connected to your spirit so that you can remember who you are and why you chose to be born into this lifetime.

For this topic, I'm going to embark upon the metaphysical realm, so for you newcomers to the subject, I am trusting that you will take this information with the love and care that I have been guided to share with you.

When I think about being in spirit, to me this isn't about religion, although if you come from a religious background, some of what I'll share will likely resonate as such, whereas perhaps some of the other thoughts may feel foreign to you or even make you a little uneasy. It is not my intent to offend. These are simply my points of view – my beliefs from the teachings and learning I have experienced over the past several years. And in my opinion, they are instrumental for a joyful life. So, let's get started.

"It is not until you change your identity to match your life blueprint that you will understand why everything in the past never worked."

~ Shannon L. Alder

I believe that we all chose to come to earth to fulfil a specific life purpose. Which means we choose when we are to be born, our parents, our culture and our life experiences as they are all are essential elements for our evolution this time around. We may not be aware of this on a conscious level, but our spirit knows.

One of my favourite books on this topic is, *The Life You Were Born to Live* by Dan Millman. This book really helped me integrate various principles I had learned through my study of numerology and astrology and clearly articulated the focus areas, specific to me, that would assist my journey.

Millman's book showed me how to calculate my birth number and then gave me insight into my personality and my life-path. It was uncannily accurate and on a soul level, I knew immediately that it spoke the truth – for me. I then went on to study numerology in more detail with Vikki McKinnon – www.gotyournumber.ca and regularly refer to these teachings to provide insights and guidance for daily living.

"The first peace, which is the most important, is that which comes within the souls of people when they realize their relationship, their oneness with the universe and all its powers, and when they realize at the center of the universe dwells the Great Spirit, and that its center is really everywhere, it is within each of us."
~ Black Elk

One of the best ways I've found to connect to my spirit is through silence and meditation. That's when you turn your brain off and turn your heart and soul on – that's when you listen to Spirit's messages.

And truly one of the best places to do this is outside, surrounded by Mother Nature's living energy of plants, flowers and trees – especially trees. And that brings me to the subject of today's activity of tree hugging.

Not only can hugging a tree improve concentration, diminish depression and even help with headaches, because of the tree's high vibration, it can do even more.

You may already be aware that our world is entirely made up of energy. In fact, everything vibrates with energy. So, when you are surrounded by things that have high vibrational energy, you will naturally be affected by those vibes. And when you are in high vibration, not only feeling good physically and emotionally, you can then tap into your own soul's energy – your true essence. That's really being in-spirit.

I ran across a great article online that referenced NatureAndHealth.com for this tidbit of information that helps reinforce my point: "In Japan, people practise 'forest bathing,' where they spend quiet time absorbing the wisdom of ancient forests, taking long walks among the trees to stimulate their immune system. In Taoism, students are encouraged to meditate among trees, and it is believed that the trees will absorb negative energies, replacing them with healthy ones. Trees are seen as a source of emotional and physical healing, and themselves as meditators, absorbing universal energies."

Today I encourage you to go to the forest and hug a tree, meditate on your life-purpose and tune into your soul for insight into your divine spirit. You'll know when you're living in-spirit by the amount of peace and calm you feel. And that my friend, is joyful living.

Day 19

MY DAILY AFFIRMATION

I'm connected to Spirit
in all that I do.
My heart is my compass
for joy coming through.

MY DAILY ACTIVITY

HUG A TREE: Yes, that's what I said. Find a tree today, in a forest if you can, and wrap your arms around the tree. Better still, if it's warm enough, sit with your back against the tree and feel Mother Nature's energy pulse throughout your body. In Matthew Silverstone's book *Blinded by Science,* he writes about the vibrational properties of trees to assist with depression, concentration, and headaches. A wonderful way to help your body and connect to your spirit.

MY DAILY FREQUENCY SHIFTER

At the end of each day, rate your state of joy on this **Joy-meter** *and then make any comments or observations about your feelings during the day or about anything noteworthy that occurred. This will help you see how your joy increases during the 40 days and what "shows up" for you.*

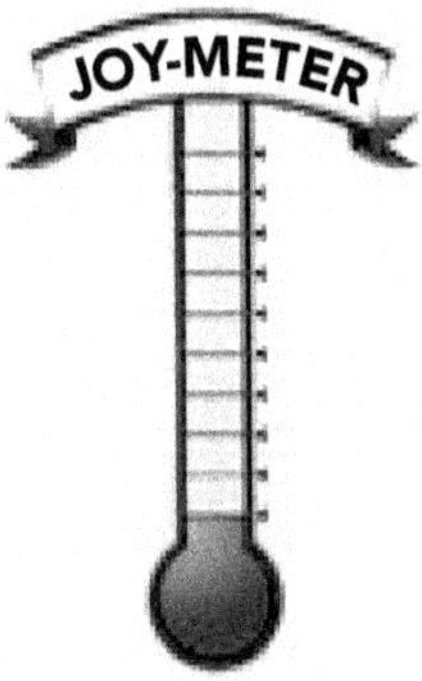

10 – Off the charts.
9 – Super amazing.
8 – Pretty blissful.
7 – Oh happy joy.
6 – I believe.
5 – I've turned the corner.
4 – I'm breathing easier.
3 – I can see the light.
2 – The clouds are lifting.
1 – I feel depressed.

NOTES

Day 19

Day 20

BE GENEROUS

*"Thousands of candles can be lit from a single candle,
and the life of the candle will not be shortened.
Happiness never decreases by being shared."*

~ Buddha

Congratulations. You have reached the half-way point in your *40-Day Being Joy* journey. Are you beginning to feel a shift in how you feel? If you've been reading the daily chapters and doing the suggested activities, you should be on your way. If not, don't worry. I'm here with you for the next half.

I love the topic of generosity because it represents so much more than giving of your time, talent, and treasure. It's about living in a state of generosity of spirit. For when you live in this state, you return to your true nature – on the look-out for opportunities to serve. It's the place where you feel the most secure and fulfilled. It's a place of pure love and joy.

"The way you get meaning into your life is to devote yourself to loving others, devote yourself to your community around you, and devote yourself to creating something that gives you purpose and meaning."

~ Mitch Albom

True generosity of spirit is fundamentally about giving and sharing. To be generous of spirit means to be fully open to the world around you – to see where there is a need and fill it. That could be to give to another person or to a project or cause you believe in. When you allow yourself to be of service you expand life for yourself and others.

Too often people think of generosity as only being in financial terms – making a generous donation or giving a generous gift to someone. But true generosity really is about spirit. It is love manifest in your words and deeds towards the world around you. True generosity means leaving the world a better place because of your presence. And we are all capable of doing that.

"The fragrance always remains on the hand that gives the rose."
~ Gandhi

When I give to someone or something, I honestly feel better. I've found that one of the best ways to end your pity-party is to give to someone else. However, for it to stick you should only give when it's sincere and without agenda. Otherwise you risk feeling resentful, guilty, or even anxious if there is an expectation of reciprocation. True generosity of spirit comes from the Divine and needs to be given with pure intention and no expectation.

And let's not forget that you need to give to yourself first. Yes, I mean first. If you're not valuing yourself as worthy of receiving, then the generosity you extend towards others will block the flow of energy that must naturally return to you.

As Deepak Chopra says, in his book, *The Seven Spiritual Laws of Success:* "The universe operates through dynamic exchange – giving and receiving are different aspects of the flow of energy in the universe. And in our willingness to give that which we seek, we keep the abundance of the universe circulating in our lives."

So today, look for opportunities to practice generosity of spirit – to yourself and others. They are all around you if you look hard enough. It could be as simple as a smile to a stranger or as grand as going out of your way to ease the burden of someone else. All gestures of love matter. Because you matter. And that is joyful living.

Day 20

MY DAILY AFFIRMATION

I share of myself.
Where a need is, I fill it.
I matter to others,
with love I commit.

MY DAILY ACTIVITY

LET SOMEONE KNOW THEY MATTER: Write a letter to a family member or friend that you haven't talked to in a while and let them know how much they mean to you. Don't text or email. Find some nice stationery and write it in pen and mail it. You'll make someone's day when they open their mailbox and read your heartfelt words.

MY DAILY FREQUENCY SHIFTER

At the end of each day, rate your state of joy on this **Joy-meter** *and then make any comments or observations about your feelings during the day or about anything noteworthy that occurred. This will help you see how your joy increases during the 40 days and what "shows up" for you.*

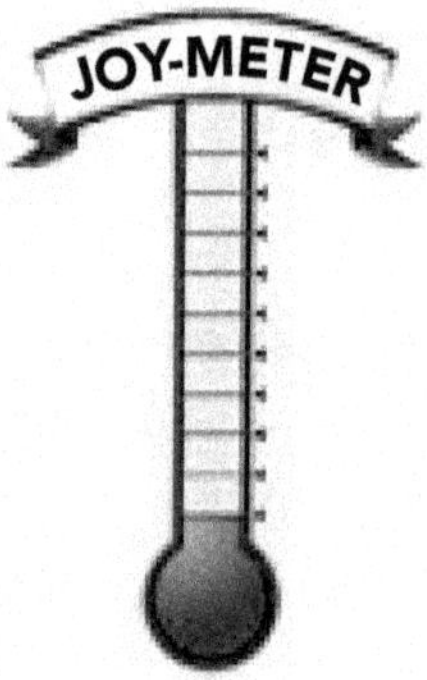

10 – Off the charts.
9 – Super amazing.
8 – Pretty blissful.
7 – Oh happy joy.
6 – I believe.
5 – I've turned the corner.
4 – I'm breathing easier.
3 – I can see the light.
2 – The clouds are lifting.
1 – I feel depressed.

NOTES

MORE NOTES

Day 21

BE RESPECTFUL

"The first duty of love is to listen."

~Paul Tillich

If you ask most people – husbands, wives, children, employees, or friends – they will tell you what they most want is respect. And to feel respected, you must first feel heard.

Paul Tillich said it best, "In my experience, I have found that people who are quick to lash out, to judge, or to be boastful are usually those who are just really insecure or afraid of losing something. They likely don't feel 'heard' in their lives and because of that they just shout louder as if to say – 'look at me – love me – look at me.'"

So instead of getting pulled into that negative and meaningless energy zone when someone does that in your company, take a deep breath and show compassion by listening and showing respect. You will honour yourself and others in the process.

"We are sun and moon, dear friend; we are sea and land. It is not our purpose to become each other; it is to recognize each other, to learn to see the other and honor him for what he is: each the other's opposite and complement."

~ Hermann Hesse

As with many of the other daily topics during this joy journey, the starting place with respect is with self. Remember, you can't give what you don't have.

Begin by learning to listen to yourself – to what your body says when you are feeling something because of someone or some experience. The body simply doesn't lie. It will tell you when someone or something isn't in your best interest. Many people use "muscle-testing" as a way of determining if a certain food product or other item is good for them or not. Others have learned how to tune into their bodies to avoid situations or environments that could be harmful. You can learn to do this too.

Have you ever walked into a room and immediately felt uncomfortable? Your stomach tightens, your throat feels constricted. Perhaps you even feel a little light-headed? That's your body reacting to the room's energy. Pay attention to it. You're not imagining it.

Your body will generally let you know loud and clear – usually with the onset of a cold or other illness – when you haven't been respecting its signals. Don't dismiss this as simply catching a virus. Your body is trying to tell you that something's off.

Self-respect is about honouring your body temple as well as how you allow yourself to be treated by others. It's about honouring your feelings as well as your hopes and dreams. It's about respect for your entire being – physically, emotionally, mentally, and spiritually. If you're not respecting yourself, not only will you make it difficult for others to respect you, but you won't be able to show genuine respect for others.

Remember that giving respect also gives dignity. And that's something we all deserve and can use more of these days. And that is joyful living.

Day 21

MY DAILY AFFIRMATION

When I respect myself
then I am truly free
to honour truth in others
and joy will come to me.

MY DAILY ACTIVITY

LISTEN: Be a mindful listener today. Truly listen as others speak to you today. Resist the temptation to interrupt or to try to tell them what they should do. Just hold space for them and listen with your heart. And don't forget to listen to yourself – to what your body is telling you. Tune in – your true self is waiting to be heard.

MY DAILY FREQUENCY SHIFTER

At the end of each day, rate your state of joy on this **Joy-meter** *and then make any comments or observations about your feelings during the day or about anything noteworthy that occurred. This will help you see how your joy increases during the 40 days and what "shows up" for you.*

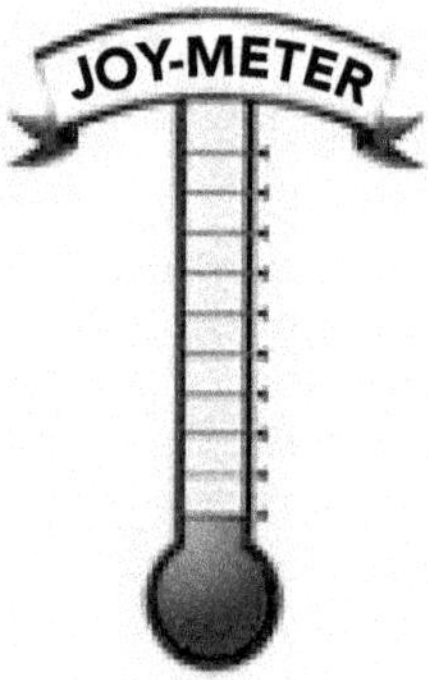

10 – Off the charts.
9 – Super amazing.
8 – Pretty blissful.
7 – Oh happy joy.
6 – I believe.
5 – I've turned the corner.
4 – I'm breathing easier.
3 – I can see the light.
2 – The clouds are lifting.
1 – I feel depressed.

NOTES

____

____

____

____

____

____

____

____

____

____

____

Day 21

MORE NOTES

Day 22

BE BELIEVING

"As a seed buried in the earth cannot imagine itself as an orchid or hyacinth, neither can a heart packed by hurt imagine itself loved or at peace. The courage of the seed is that once cracking, it cracks all the way."

~ Mark Nepo

If you haven't gathered by now, I love quotes. I have discovered such profound poetic wisdom through quotes by women and men who have bared their vulnerability to share their true thoughts. And occasionally, I land across a great one that stays with me.

You have likely heard this one. I'm not even sure who originally said it, but it goes, "You don't see the world the way it is. You see the world the way you are." It's all about how your beliefs shape your reality. And because you are one hundred percent responsible for your experience in life, it's so important to examine how your beliefs can either serve you or get in your way.

But where do your beliefs come from? Many are formed early in life – most you adopt from your parents and extended families. Your friends and peers shape a great deal of them. Religion plays a significant role for many people.

We are attracted to people who share the same beliefs as we do – the same way of seeing the world, the same likes and dislikes. Then we go to school and many of our beliefs start to shift. We marry, have children, age, and our beliefs shift again as we change. Or do we change because of our beliefs? Both, I would say.

I think sometimes people confuse beliefs with values. To me, values are the core of who you are – they are the principles by which you live – they are the fundamentals and usually do not change. Beliefs on the other hand do and should. You may believe something one day, then learn new facts or have different experiences that change your beliefs for the future. That is the basis of your evolution.

So, let's talk a bit about how being attached to your beliefs can interfere with your ability to live a joyful life.

"Someone asked us recently, 'Is there any limitation to the body's ability to heal?' And we said, None, other than the belief that you hold. And he asks, 'Then why aren't people growing new limbs?' And we said, Because no one believes they can."
~Abraham Hicks

I was recently asked to make a presentation about belief attachments to a group who was participating in a Sacred Women's retreat. Much of my learning about this subject came from Don Miguel Ruiz Jr in his book, *The Five Levels of Attachment*, and I highly recommend you read it if you are interested in delving deeper into this topic.

I learned how to identify the attachments we have to specific beliefs we hold and how to change those that limit us. Ruiz taught me that it's really about seeing and living beyond our filters – our accumulated knowledge and beliefs.

You see, we have spent years becoming attached to certain beliefs that begin to shape our future experience and limit us. Like wearing blinders, you can limit your vision and this in turn can limit your direction in life. It can cause great suffering if you are rigidly attached and limit your experiences. (I've seen this most dramatically in people who are attached to religion, money, and fame.) Simply put, attachment to your beliefs will block the flow of your soul's intention.

"If you don't change your beliefs,
your life will be like this forever.
Is that good news?"
~ W. Somerset Maugham

So, that's all I'm going to say about beliefs from the standpoint of attachment. I only bring this up because I want you to be aware that *it's the choices you make about the stories you tell yourself based on your beliefs that dictate the experiences you will have.* And once you reflect on that, you'll understand that you are one hundred percent responsible for what shows up in your life. And if you don't like what's showing up, look to a belief that you hold for some insight.

I'll close today's chapter by giving you another great quote that goes, "You have to believe it before you can see it." What do you believe? What do you want to see? I'm going to assume since you've read this far, that you want more joy. For joy is the gateway to receiving more wonderful things in your life.

Believe in and practice joyfulness each and every day and you will see it unfold all around you – it's that simple. Just be the joy you want to see. And that my friend, is joyful living.

Day 22

MY DAILY AFFIRMATION

I see the world as loving and giving.
I believe in myself and that life is worth living.
I create my own world by the way that I feel
and my practice of joy has the power to heal.

MY DAILY ACTIVITY

WISH LIST: Make a wish list of all the things you would like to have in the coming year. They could be material things or improvements in relationships or things you would like to change about yourself. Once you have completed the list, read it once through, bless it and give thanks. Then tuck it under your pillow tonight with the belief that it is already done.

MY DAILY FREQUENCY SHIFTER

At the end of each day, rate your state of joy on this ***Joy-meter*** *and then make any comments or observations about your feelings during the day or about anything noteworthy that occurred. This will help you see how your joy increases during the 40 days and what "shows up" for you.*

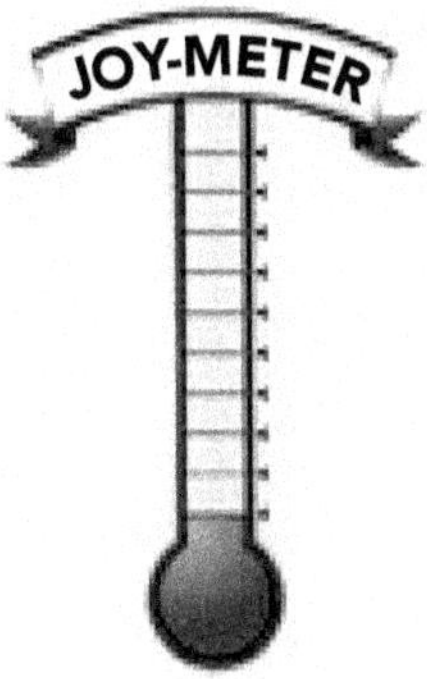

10 – Off the charts.
9 – Super amazing.
8 – Pretty blissful.
7 – Oh happy joy.
6 – I believe.
5 – I've turned the corner.
4 – I'm breathing easier.
3 – I can see the light.
2 – The clouds are lifting.
1 – I feel depressed.

NOTES

Day 22

Day 23

BE ABUNDANT

"Abundance is not something we acquire.
It is something we tune in to."

~ Wayne Dyer

Today's topic is going to help you "tune in" to your abundance after outlining some key factors that are likely getting in the way of you having it right now. And "being abundant" is such an important ingredient for joyful living. So, get ready.

The challenge we face today is that many people have been taught to believe that life is difficult. And we've been conditioned to look out for number one. We've been told that we must get it first before someone else does because there's not enough.

If you're like most people right now, you've been subjected to a culture of fear and scarcity – whether it's related to a lack of money, love, time, or anything else for that matter. You've bought into the illusion that there's a shortage of those things. That's right – it's an illusion.

Let's look at some beliefs you may be attached to that are contributing to your feeling of scarcity and then we can look at what you can do to turn that around.

Belief #1 – There's not enough

According to Lynne Twist in her remarkable book *The Soul of Money,* the reality is that our planet is actually overflowing with abundance. Having been impacted by the teachings of, and friendship with Buckminster Fuller more than forty years ago, Lynne said in her book that Fuller relayed to her that "...at this point in history – in the 1970s we were able to do so much more with so much less that as a human family we clearly had reached a point where there actually was enough for everyone everywhere to meet or even surpass their needs to live a reasonably healthy, productive life." So please put that belief of lack to rest. Your abundance can't arrive when you're in a state of panic and worry – fear blocks flow.

Belief #2 – I'm not worthy.

Louise Hay says that the root of most of our problems in life are contained in the feeling *I'm not good enough.* This is one of the biggest and most commonly-held beliefs, especially among women. Women generally put themselves last, are poor receivers, suffer in silence, and are then distressed when abundance doesn't flow to them as they think it should.

> ***"Do you think I ultimately reward those who live in poverty? Do you think those who toil and sweat from paycheck to paycheck are more likely to inherit the Kingdom than those who work in ivory towers? Do you think I take special notice of sacrifices? That I'm pleased when some put the needs of others before their own? Or that I favour those who strive to live spiritual lives? Actually, I don't give a flying yahoo – I love you no matter what rules you make up."***
>
> ~ Mike Dooley – The Universe

Belief #3. I don't want to be like the filthy rich anyway.

When it comes to attracting prosperity, you really need to look at the firmly-held beliefs about money that are running in your life to understand why it's not flowing to you. Some of this may even be unconscious.

For example, do you believe that rich people are stingy or phony? Do you use the term "filthy rich" when you speak of wealthy people? How about adages like, "You have to work hard to make money," or "Money doesn't grow on trees," or "The rich get richer and the poor get poorer" How about "You should have just enough to get by, otherwise you're greedy." And my personal favourite, "Money doesn't buy happiness."

Can you see what you might be doing by holding onto these judgements? You're basically saying, "I don't want to be like that, so don't bring me any of that filthy money." No wonder it's not showing up for you.

Believe #4 – It is what it is – I can't change things.

This is where you believe it's too hard, you're too old, you didn't have the same opportunities as others, you're not good-looking enough, you don't know enough, and besides, not everyone can have it all. Again, you're telling the Universe that you really don't want abundance to flow to you. You're o.k. with the way things are.

"You do not have to have money to attract money, but you cannot feel poor and attract money. The key is, you have to find ways of improving the way you feel from right where you stand before things can begin to change. By softening your attention to the things that are going wrong, and by beginning to tell stories that lean more in the direction of what you want instead of in the direction of what you have got, your vibration will shift; your point of attraction will shift–and you will get different results."

~Abraham Hicks

Day 23

Belief #5 – I'm not lucky– poor me.

If this is you, I would encourage you to go back and re-read Chapter 15 on acceptance. Being a victim in your life reinforces your belief that life happens to you. You've given all your power away. You focus on obstacles, never take risks for fear of failing, you think small and get stuck in your story. Abundance simply can't flow to a victim because a victim is not living in a vibration that would ever see the opportunities.

Belief #6 – I must be in control.

By now, I hope I've sufficiently emphasized the message of letting go so that you can open yourself up to receiving that which you want. As counter-intuitive as it may seem, this really is the key. You absolutely must release control to allow the flow of abundance to come to you. Again, go back and review Chapter 8 on release and Chapter 13 on accepting if you need some further reinforcement on this.

When your belief tells you that you must be in control, that's just your ego talking because it doesn't want you to veer off into the unknown. Ego likes security. But control is fear-based. The more you struggle to attract your desire, the more you push it away, because the energy you're creating is focused on what you don't have instead of what you do. Remember, it isn't your job to make it happen. *It's your job to allow it to happen.* So, relax and let it.

I hope today's chapter has helped you examine some beliefs you hold that are preventing you from living in a joyful state of plenty. Remember, you set the course for your next "prosperous" experience. And that is joyful living.

Day 23

MY DAILY AFFIRMATION

I always know I'll have enough
that Spirit won't forsake me.
Through love and joy, attraction works.
Surrender sets me free.

MY DAILY ACTIVITY

MAIL YOURSELF A CHEQUE: Write yourself an "abundance cheque" for whatever amount you want, and then mail it to yourself. Open it and tape it to your wall along with the envelope it came in. Make the amount believable to you but also a stretch. It's the combination of belief and focused intention that when written with joy and not desperation, holds great power.

MY DAILY FREQUENCY SHIFTER

At the end of each day, rate your state of joy on this **Joy-meter** *and then make any comments or observations about your feelings during the day or about anything noteworthy that occurred. This will help you see how your joy increases during the 40 days and what "shows up" for you.*

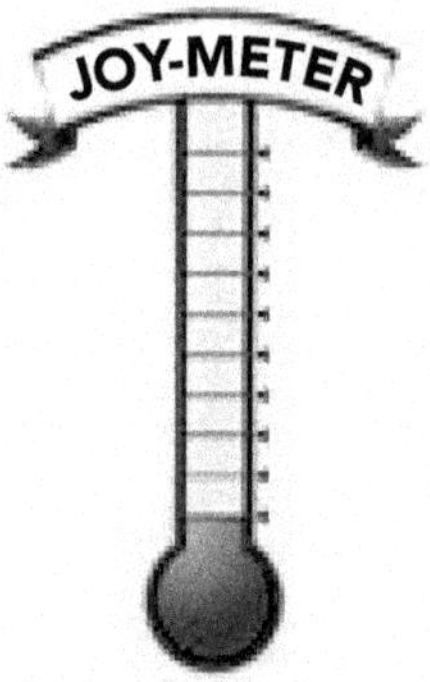

10 – Off the charts.
9 – Super amazing.
8 – Pretty blissful.
7 – Oh happy joy.
6 – I believe.
5 – I've turned the corner.
4 – I'm breathing easier.
3 – I can see the light.
2 – The clouds are lifting.
1 – I feel depressed.

NOTES

Day 23

MORE NOTES

Day 24

BE IN BALANCE

"Balance, peace, and joy are the fruit of a successful life. It starts with recognizing your talents and finding ways to serve others by using them."

~Thomas Kinkade

We talk a lot these days about "being in balance," balancing our home and work life, about feeling balanced. What does that really mean?

For example, you can look at one person's life where they may work twelve hours a day and only sleep six hours a night and make the judgement that they are not living in balance.

Then you look at another person who only works three or four hours a day and sleeps eight to nine hours a night and determine that they must be living a much more balanced life than the first example.

But what if the first person absolutely loves what they do? They don't stress easily, have quality relationships with friends and family, and sleep peacefully. Whereas the second person hates their job, is anxious about money all the time, and is estranged from their family. Who is living a more balanced life?

The purpose of these examples is to show you that you can never determine what balance is by looking at the lives of others. So, don't judge yourself by looking at what you think is working or not working for someone else. You can only look at yourself, your own state of being, and determine if you feel balanced, joyful, and whole or not.

"Problems arise in that one has to find a balance between what people need from you and what you need for yourself."

~ Jessye Norman

The test is, how do you feel? Do you resent what you do for a living? If you're a busy mom, are you feeling worn out and unappreciated? If you're retired, are you feeling a lack of purpose? The amount of sleep you get, and the amount of recreation time really have very little to do with whether you are living in balance or not. It's really about how you feel about what you do that matters.

Now don't get me wrong. Adequate sleep, proper nutrition, and "down" time are important for your physical and emotional well-being. But far too often we minimize the importance of nurturing relationships with family and friends, fun time, and life purpose.

The peace of mind you feel right now will tell you whether you are in balance or not. And if you're not, let's talk about what you can do to change that.

"With an eye made quiet by the power of harmony, and the deep power of joy, we see into the life of things."
~ William Wordsworth

As with so many other realizations, the first step is admitting that you aren't where you want to be and then making the commitment to detach from some of your tightly-held beliefs that likely got you here. If you need to go back and refresh yourself on the power of beliefs, re-read Chapter 22. So, let's break down some examples.

Let's say you are a busy working mom. You chose to go back to work believing that you could do it all, single-handed. You watched your mom raise three children on her own and if she could do it, you could too. And besides, you have a husband to help out. But that's not what happened, was it?

You aren't getting enough sleep, your job requires that you stay late on too many nights, you're getting into arguments with your husband, and you never have enough time with the kids or to just sit down and read a book. You are starting to feel inadequate in all areas of your life. But because you are attached to the belief that moms and wives are supposed to behave a certain way, you don't ask for help.

But what if you just loosened your grip a bit and let go? What if at work you delegated some of your responsibilities to your staff? And at home you asked your husband to pitch in more – sure the dishwasher may not be loaded just the way you do it, but remember from Chapter 15, "good enough is good enough." What if you sat down and really examined some of your beliefs about motherhood and family life that no longer serve the life you are building within your own family? What if the new goal becomes balance and joy instead of the unrealistic expectations you have held onto because of your beliefs?

"Be really whole and all things will come to you."

~ Lao-Tzu

One more example. Let's say you have recently retired. You believe retirement is a time when you don't have to set your alarm clock anymore and your time is your own. You think that you'll have lots of time to pursue your hobbies and visit friends and family. But what you didn't take into consideration is that your friends and family have their own lives. They aren't retired so they are still busy working and creating their own experiences. You begin to feel unwanted.

Your hobbies no longer interest you and you become lonely, waiting for the phone to ring. You find yourself sleeping ten hours a night and staying home for days on end. You become depressed and isolated. You aren't living in balance and harmony. And you feel very little joy…all because retirement didn't turn out the way you "believed" it should.

Remember, you are one hundred percent responsible for what shows up in your life. And your beliefs drive that. So, if you aren't living a happy and balanced life, you need to re-define your life. You get to choose what it looks like for you – not because of or for anyone else. And when you do that, you will discover that is joyful living.

Day 24

MY DAILY AFFIRMATION

Everything's in harmony.
My body's calm and grounded.
Things around me – as they should.
All is well and balanced.

MY DAILY ACTIVITY

BALANCING CHALLENGE: To physically demonstrate the importance of overall balance – mind, body, and spirit, try this exercise. Find a place in your room where you can stand and stretch out your arms. Stand on one leg and hold your arms out beside you for thirty seconds. Then stand on the other leg for thirty seconds with your arms above your head. Close your eyes while standing and breathe deeply if you can. If not, with eyes open, breathe peacefully. Repeat three times today.

MY DAILY FREQUENCY SHIFTER

At the end of each day, rate your state of joy on this **Joy-meter** *and then make any comments or observations about your feelings during the day or about anything noteworthy that occurred. This will help you see how your joy increases during the 40 days and what "shows up" for you.*

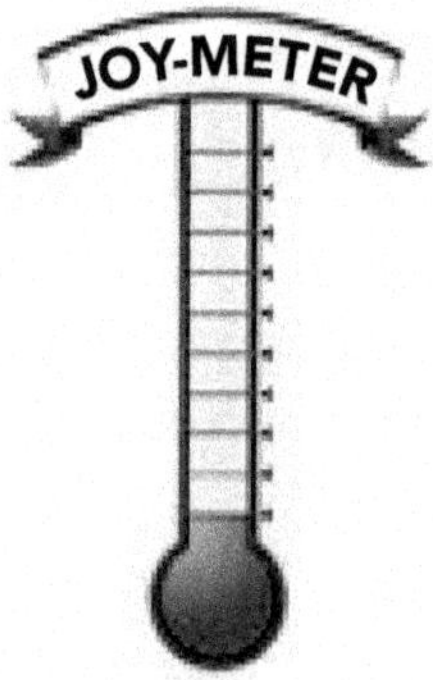

10 – Off the charts.
9 – Super amazing.
8 – Pretty blissful.
7 – Oh happy joy.
6 – I believe.
5 – I've turned the corner.
4 – I'm breathing easier.
3 – I can see the light.
2 – The clouds are lifting.
1 – I feel depressed.

NOTES

Day 24

MORE NOTES

Day 25

BE FORGIVING

"Forgiveness is looking at people with the spiritual knowledge of their innocence rather than the mortal perception of their guilt."

~Marianne Williamson

We've all had experiences of feeling slighted. We've had friends or family do or say things that hurt our feelings or perhaps had someone harm us in a deeply emotional or physical way. Relationships are tricky. And it often seems that the ones closest to us are the ones who hurt us the most.

I'm sure you've heard stories of brothers who haven't seen each other in years, of a mother and daughter who no longer speak, or of best friends who had a falling out and family feuds that have gone on for several generations. And all the while, bitterness and resentment continue to fester, and lives are forever shattered.

"Forgiveness does not change the past, but it does enlarge the future."

~ Paul Boese

Forgiving someone who has wounded you may be a painful choice and may not come easily. But at the end of the day, once you've wrestled with all the reasons why you shouldn't forgive that person or why you were right, and they were wrong, it simply doesn't matter. Remember, forgiveness does not mean that you're condoning someone else's behaviour. It simply means you are freeing yourself from carrying the memory of that hurt within you.

For to forgive someone is not really a gift you give to someone else. It is a gift you give yourself. In fact, the word "forgive" means both to give and receive – to *"give for."*

Forgiveness releases the toxic energy you've been holding onto so tightly out of indignation or stubbornness and makes a new space for self-love, patience, understanding, and joy. But like everything else in this life, it's a choice. Remember, what happens in your life is not your fault, but it is your responsibility.

Now let's talk about self-forgiveness, because as we've already discussed a few times throughout this journey, you can't give what you don't have.

"Sometimes in order to be happy in the present moment you have to be willing to give up all hope for a better past."
~ Robert Holden

Why are we so hard on ourselves? Why do so many of us believe we must suffer because of past mistakes we have made? Why do we hold onto them, punishing ourselves repeatedly? It's like guilt and self-loathing have been hard-wired into our psyche. And for many of us, they have.

Be it through religious doctrine, family conditioning or rigid beliefs held about perfectionism, millions of people are so haunted by their own perceived transgressions, they block the flow of joy. Please, my dear beloved reader, forgive yourself now. Instead of being sorry, commit to being better.

"Forgiveness is the fragrance that the violet sheds on the heel that has crushed it."
~ Mark Twain

There is an alchemy in forgiveness that is quite profound and magical. And if you're interested in going a little deeper into this subject, I would like to briefly introduce you to an interesting Hawaiian system called ho'oponopono.

As described by Dr. Hew Len, a master teacher of this system, in the book, *Zero Limits* by Joe Vitale, "Simply put, ho'oponopono means to 'make right' or 'to rectify an error.' Ho'o means 'cause' in Hawaiian, ponopono means 'perfection.' According to the ancient Hawaiians, error arises from thoughts that are tainted by painful memories from the past. Ho'oponopono offers a way to release the energy of these painful thoughts, or errors, which cause imbalance and disease."

Here is the simple but powerful prayer of forgiveness.

I am sorry. Please forgive me. I Love you, Thank-you.

This is a fascinating method of release, forgiveness, and love and it's one that I thought you might be interested in doing a bit more research on. Of course, there are many other methods to assist you in releasing the past so that you can move forward. If you are feeling really stuck in this area, you may want to seek out the services of a trained professional. It could be that some of these memories are from another lifetime or are even a result of various ancestral attachments, so working with a shaman or other spiritual professional may be of help to you.

In the meantime, I'll close today by asking you to start by showing compassion towards yourself and others. Anger, defensiveness, martyrdom, and so forth do not attract miracles. Mercy and compassion do. And that is joyful living.

Day 25

MY DAILY AFFIRMATION

Today the gift I give myself
will grow my joy forever.
It's forgiveness that will heal all wounds
and mend my heart together.

MY DAILY ACTIVITY

WRITE A FORGIVENESS LETTER: Write a letter to yourself or someone else that you have had difficulty forgiving. Unleash your feelings about the situation and at the end say, "I Forgive You." Then as you fold the paper, say a prayer of release, and then burn the letter. You have given your prayer to the Universe and released your burden of resentment. This is a very powerful activity that you can do anytime you need to forgive yourself or someone else.

MY DAILY FREQUENCY SHIFTER

At the end of each day, rate your state of joy on this ***Joy-meter*** *and then make any comments or observations about your feelings during the day or about anything noteworthy that occurred. This will help you see how your joy increases during the 40 days and what "shows up" for you.*

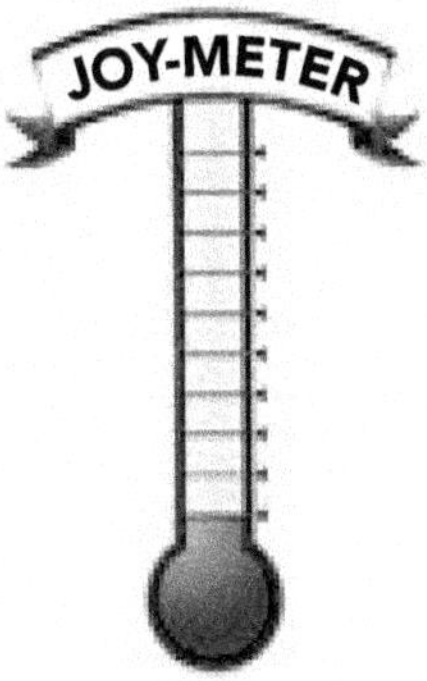

10 – Off the charts.
9 – Super amazing.
8 – Pretty blissful.
7 – Oh happy joy.
6 – I believe.
5 – I've turned the corner.
4 – I'm breathing easier.
3 – I can see the light.
2 – The clouds are lifting.
1 – I feel depressed.

NOTES

Day 25

Day 26

BE HAPPY

"Young souls learn to accept responsibility for their actions.
Mature souls learn to accept responsibility for their thoughts.
And old souls learn to accept responsibility for their happiness."

~ Mike Dooley

As I suggested in my letter at the beginning of this book, I see happiness and joy as being two different things. Happiness is generally something that happens because of something, whereas joy is a state of being. Because of that I want to focus on the topic of happiness in today's chapter so that you can see that you have power in driving your own happiness, which will help you live more joyfully.

Like I've said repeatedly, you are one hundred percent responsible for everything that happens in your life. And that applies to your happiness too. It all depends on how you think and how you choose to react to things that happen in your life.

Do you see yourself as a glass half-full or as a glass half-empty person? As simple as that question is, it can reveal a lot about how you see the world and ultimately the experiences you attract.

Do you believe you deserve happiness? What does happiness look like to you? Are you living it now? These are important questions to ask yourself as they provide valuable insight into your current attitudes towards happiness.

"Be happy for no reason, like a child. If you are happy for a reason, you're in trouble, because that reason can be taken from you."

~ Deepak Chopra

I hear so many people say, "When I get that new house I'll be happy," or "As soon as I retire and start travelling I'll be happy," or "When I win the big one I'll be happy." But if you break it down, you'll see that the end-goal really isn't the stuff or the status or the money. The end goal is happiness. So why not choose that first?

As we talked about in Chapter 23 on abundance, if you want more abundance, then be abundant – smile and feel it throughout your entire being. Don't wait for something to happen to feel it. Feel happy first. By doing that, you create the vibration that will attract more happiness and then more happiness. And soon the stuff will become irrelevant because you've achieved the end goal. Does that make sense to you? No? O.k. let's keep going.

> ***"The trick is in what one emphasizes.***
> ***We either make ourselves miserable,***
> ***or we make ourselves happy.***
> ***The amount of work is the same."***
> ~ Carlos Castaneda

I keep bringing up the Law of Attraction. You may think that it's a bunch of new-age hooey, but it's actually a concept that's been around for more than a century and is scientifically sound. It operates upon the principle that everything is made up of energy – you, me, all life, everything. And it's our vibrational frequency that attracts back to us more of the same.

So, when you feel like a victim, or are unhappy or judgemental, you'll attract experiences that mirror your feelings. Whereas when your frequency is high through feelings of love and joy, you attract more love and joy back into your life. That's putting it very simplistically, but quite frankly, it's not that difficult a concept. Don't overthink it. Trust that it's legit. And if you're not sure, then do some more research on your own.

"There is no duty we so much underrate as the duty of being happy. By being happy we sow anonymous benefits upon the world."
~ Robert Louis Stevenson

I believe we need more happiness in our world. There is plenty of sadness and fear lurking at every corner, on every TV channel and every newspaper. Don't buy into it. Collectively, we have the power and I believe the responsibility, to shift the frequency of the world by shifting our own happiness frequency. And that is joyful living.

Day 26

MY DAILY AFFIRMATION

Today I sit as still can be
and let the peace flow through me.
I feel the love that shifts my heart.
I smile as joy comes to me.

MY DAILY ACTIVITY

YOUR HAPPINESS LIST: Make a list of all the things that make you happy. Make it as long as you can. Review it during the day and add to it. Then when you find yourself in a sad place, pull out your list and read it until you start to feel the joy return.

Or try another method called tapping. In Donna Eden's book *Energy Medicine,* she says, "The next time you feel fabulous, riveted, connected, on a high, or otherwise happy, reinforce this energy by 'tapping' the joy at your third eye, the point between your eyebrows just above the bridge of your nose. Tap with a steady beat for ten to twelve seconds." Give it a try.

MY DAILY FREQUENCY SHIFTER

At the end of each day, rate your state of joy on this **Joy-meter** *and then make any comments or observations about your feelings during the day or about anything noteworthy that occurred. This will help you see how your joy increases during the 40 days and what "shows up" for you.*

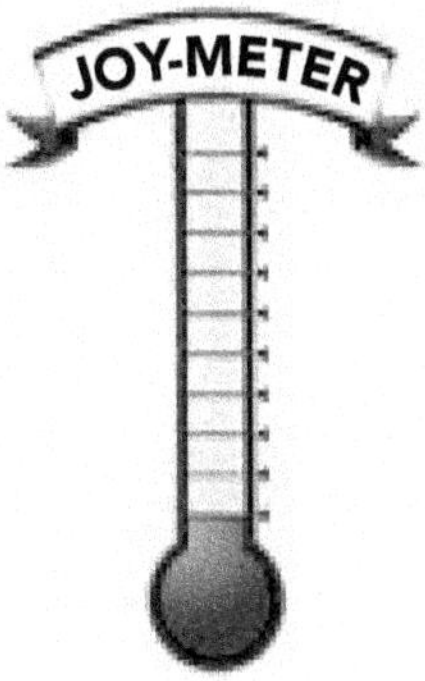

10 – Off the charts.
9 – Super amazing.
8 – Pretty blissful.
7 – Oh happy joy.
6 – I believe.
5 – I've turned the corner.
4 – I'm breathing easier.
3 – I can see the light.
2 – The clouds are lifting.
1 – I feel depressed.

NOTES

Day 26

Day 27

BE HOPEFUL

"When the world says, 'Give up,'
Hope whispers, 'Try it one more time.'"

~ Author Unknown

A few years ago, I ran across a very interesting charitable organization while travelling on business. I was so curious about them, that I stopped in to learn more. They are The Hope Foundation of Alberta and if you look at their website, they are "dedicated to the study and enhancement of hope." They have joined forces with the University of Alberta and do "hope" research as well as offering counselling services and workshops and providing useful information about the importance of hope. Check out their website at www.ualberta.ca/HOPE if you're interested in learning more.

This "chance" meeting led me to do more exploration about hope. You see, I personally have experienced how important hope can be for joyful living. Not just in terms of health and healing, which is how most people tend to think of hope, but I believe hope represents empowerment. Let me explain.

When I've experienced troubling times of self-doubt or when I've been overwhelmed with a staggering workload or financial challenges, I've learned to turn to hope to pull myself out of feeling like a victim. I've changed my reality by envisioning the way I want things to be instead of the way they are in my mind at the moment. I embark upon what I call a "hope quest."

My hope quest looks like this. I get really clear about what the issue is that I'm facing. I remind myself that it's only a problem if I see it that way. I thank the situation for giving me the opportunity to practice gratitude for the learning and then immediately put the problem in the past. I imagine what my reality would look like without the problem in it. I really feel it, get excited about it, and then relax into it. At no time during this hope quest do I try and "solve" the problem by thinking of solutions. That will naturally occur later. The purpose of the quest is to shift my energy into hope and belief as if I am already living in the outcome.

"Be realistic. Plan for a miracle."
~ Osho

Hope is about focusing intently enough on your hopes and dreams that the negative energy begins to vanish. You replace the negative with the positive as you elevate your frequency to a more hopeful and joyful state. It's about having faith that you can manifest what you desire. And that's hope in action.

You see, hope is a participation sport. You can't just sit back and wait for it. It requires that you shift your feelings from lack to abundance and from despair to belief. That you take one hundred percent responsibility for your life but that you are compassionate towards yourself in the process. Just say to yourself, *"I may not be there yet, but I'm closer than I was yesterday."* That's incredibly empowering.

I'd like to share a lovely little poem about hope by Emily Dickinson. It's simple, sweet and profound.

"Hope" is the thing with feathers
That perches in the soul
And sings the tune without the words
And never stops at all
And sweetest in the Gale is heard
And sore must be the storm
That could abash the little Bird
That kept so many warm
I've heard it in the chilliest land
And on the strangest Sea
Yet, never, in Extremity,
It asked a crumb of Me."

Please, my beloved reader, if you are going through challenging times right now – if you're dealing with illness, depression, or lack, please remember that you are not alone in your transformation. You have the power to change your circumstances. Know that. Believe that. Keep your heart open and your hope alive. And that is joyful living.

Day 27

MY DAILY AFFIRMATION

Hope is here and always was.
I just can't always see it.
Today I open heart to hear
Spirit say, "believe it."

MY DAILY ACTIVITY

SOUL LETTER TO GOD: Write a soul letter to God, Spirit, Source, or Universe – whatever power you believe in, expressing what you are most troubled about. Lay it all out for God to hear. Then ask to be given a clear sign in this physical world that you have been heard, which you will notice and understand. Have faith and take inspired action as you are guided to do so.

MY DAILY FREQUENCY SHIFTER

At the end of each day, rate your state of joy on this ***Joy-meter*** *and then make any comments or observations about your feelings during the day or about anything noteworthy that occurred. This will help you see how your joy increases during the 40 days and what "shows up" for you.*

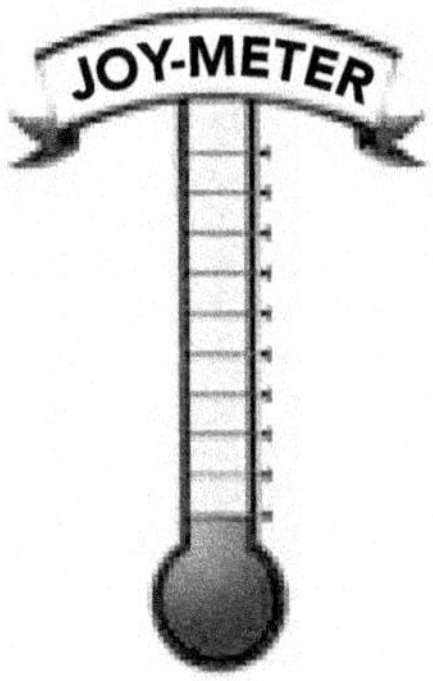

10 – Off the charts.
9 – Super amazing.
8 – Pretty blissful.
7 – Oh happy joy.
6 – I believe.
5 – I've turned the corner.
4 – I'm breathing easier.
3 – I can see the light.
2 – The clouds are lifting.
1 – I feel depressed.

NOTES

Day 27

Day 28

BE CHOOSY

"Attitude is a choice.
Happiness is a choice.
Optimism is a choice.
Kindness is a choice.
Giving is a choice.
Respect is a choice.
Whatever choice you make makes you.
Choose wisely."

~Roy T. Bennett

Choice. Most of us understand on an intellectual level, at least, the impact our choices have on our lives. But we don't often pay enough attention to the little, and sometimes more automatic, choices we make every second of the day. Our habits, the way we think, the actions we take or don't take, the words we use to communicate and so on. These little choices impact everything that will happen next in our lives.

And I believe that to live a more joyful life, you must choose joy as your natural state of being. And like everything else, it is a choice. So please don't give yours away.

"We are our choices."
~ Jean-Paul Sartre

There's a heart-warming story that I heard Wayne Dyer tell at a workshop he led many years ago. I have provided it here to illustrate the beauty and grace in living fully in a state of joy. It goes like this:

The petite, poised, and proud ninety-two-year-old lady, who even though she is legally blind is fully dressed each morning by eight o'clock with her hair fashionably coiffed and her makeup perfectly applied, moved to a nursing home today.

Her husband of seventy years recently passed away, making the move necessary.

After many hours of waiting patiently in the lobby of the nursing home, she smiled sweetly when told her room was ready. As she maneuvered her walker to the elevator, a visual description of her tiny room, including the eyelet curtains that had been hung on her window, was provided.

"I love it," she stated with the enthusiasm of an eight-year-old just presented with a new puppy.

"Mrs. Jones, you haven't seen the room...just wait."

"That doesn't have anything to do with it," she replied.

"Happiness is something you decide on ahead of time. Whether I like my room or not doesn't depend on how the furniture is arranged...it's how I arrange my mind. I already decided to love it...

"It's a decision I make every morning when I wake up. I have a choice:

I can spend my day in bed recounting the difficulties I have with the parts of my body that no longer work or get out of bed and be thankful for the ones that do. Each day is a gift, and as long as my eyes open, I'll focus on the new day and all the happy memories I've stored away...for just this time in my life.

Old age is like a bank account...you withdraw from what you've put in...so, my advice to you would be to deposit a lot of happiness in the bank account of memories.

Thank you for your part in filling my memory bank. I am still depositing."

Love this...Isn't that a great attitude? Our only goal should be happiness. Not the money or the things or the people we believe will bring us happiness. You will attract those just by being in your natural state of joy.

So today, I ask you to smile. Be present, laugh more, and pay attention to the thoughts and actions that are either moving you in the direction of joy or away from it. It's your choice. And that is joyful living.

Day 28

MY DAILY AFFIRMATION

Today my choice is joy before
I've even seen the outcome.
For when I live from what I give
true joy comes back and then some.

MY DAILY ACTIVITY

WAKING MEDITATION: This morning, before getting out of bed, spend five or ten minutes just smiling and sending loving thoughts to yourself. Then think about what you have planned for the day and choose joy first before you see the outcome. Do your best to stay in a good feeling vibe throughout the day, no matter what happens. Chances are you'll attract more good experiences than otherwise because of your choice to be happy first.

MY DAILY FREQUENCY SHIFTER

At the end of each day, rate your state of joy on this **Joy-meter** *and then make any comments or observations about your feelings during the day or about anything noteworthy that occurred. This will help you see how your joy increases during the 40 days and what "shows up" for you.*

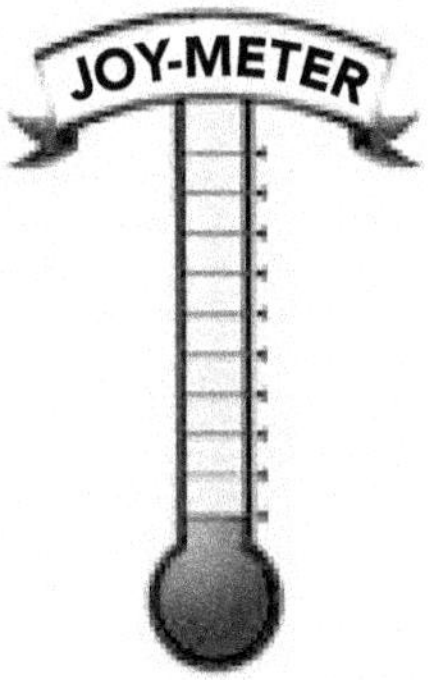

10 – Off the charts.
9 – Super amazing.
8 – Pretty blissful.
7 – Oh happy joy.
6 – I believe.
5 – I've turned the corner.
4 – I'm breathing easier.
3 – I can see the light.
2 – The clouds are lifting.
1 – I feel depressed.

NOTES

Day 28

Day 29

BE KIND

"Kind words can be short and easy to speak,
but their echoes are truly endless."

~ Mother Teresa

Do you consider yourself a kind person? Are you always kind or are there conditions? Do you withhold kindness from some people – those you might be angry with – don't agree with – don't know? Or are you kind to everyone?

Probably the best example of kindness was Mother Teresa, founder of the Order of the Missionaries of Charity, and considered one of the greatest humanitarians of the twentieth century.

Canonized as Saint Teresa of Calcutta in 2016, this mighty champion for the poor and indigent saw the light within every soul and gave fully of herself to all she met. Without judgement, Mother Teresa believed that everyone is worthy of kindness. Everyone deserves love.

> ***"Treat everyone with politeness, even those who are rude to you – not because they are nice, but because you are."***
>
> ~Author Unknown

Kindness is the giving of it and the willingness to receive it for yourself. For many people, both are difficult. What I have found is that people sometimes feel awkward showing kindness to others, particularly to strangers.

But if you believe as I do, that we are all connected, then by showing kindness to someone, you are actually loving yourself. And that brings up what I believe is the root of the issue. Lack of self-love.

You see, I feel that to show authentic generosity of spirit towards another human being, you can only do so if you are willing to receive the same love and kindness for yourself.

There are so many people in this world living in a drought of self-worth. Do you feel undeserving of praise or compassion? Are you dissatisfied with life and bitter towards others?

"A single act of kindness throws out roots in all directions, and the roots spring up and make new trees."
~Amelia Earhart

Just begin by taking a few small steps. First, accept that you are worthy of kindness and love just because you are you and you are here now.

Then, start by showing simple gestures of kindness towards others. This is even more impactful if you can do it when you are feeling the worst. I know you may not feel like it, but trust me, the best way to get out of your own "stuff" is to show kindness towards another. You see kindness and love attract more of the same. Simply put, kindness is like a boomerang. It always returns.

So today I ask you to throw your boomerang with gusto. Throw it for all to benefit, including yourself. And that my deserving reader, is joyful living.

Day 29

MY DAILY AFFIRMATION

I look in your eyes and tell you, "you matter,"
then my heart opens up to receive.
We all need each other
on this earth, our wise mother.
It is kindness and love that we seed.

MY DAILY ACTIVITY

RANDOM ACT OF KINDNESS: Today's activity is quite simple. Perform a random act of kindness for a stranger today. A smile, a compliment, a pay-it-forward coffee at the drive-through, or anything that will help to make someone else's day a little better. Don't underestimate the power of kindness to shift the joy vibration throughout the world and return it right back to you.

MY DAILY FREQUENCY SHIFTER

At the end of each day, rate your state of joy on this **Joy-meter** *and then make any comments or observations about your feelings during the day or about anything noteworthy that occurred. This will help you see how your joy increases during the 40 days and what "shows up" for you.*

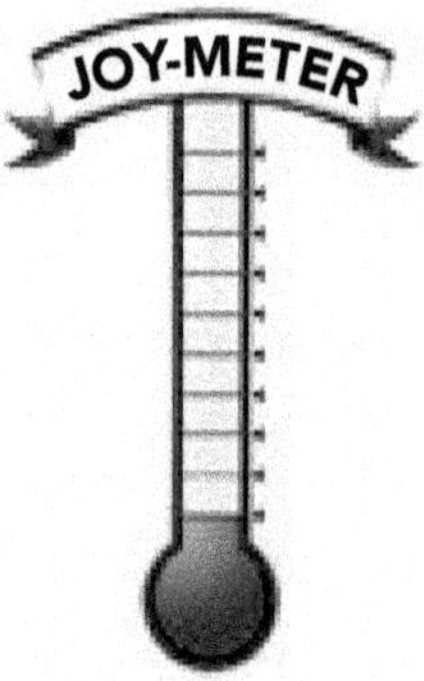

10 – Off the charts.
9 – Super amazing.
8 – Pretty blissful.
7 – Oh happy joy.
6 – I believe.
5 – I've turned the corner.
4 – I'm breathing easier.
3 – I can see the light.
2 – The clouds are lifting.
1 – I feel depressed.

NOTES

Day 29

MORE NOTES

Day 30

BE ON PURPOSE

"Don't ask what the world needs.
Ask what makes you come alive and go do it.
Because what the world needs
is people who have come alive."

~ Howard Thurman

Mark Twain said, "The two most important days in your life are the day you are born and the day you find out why."

Do you feel that you are currently living on purpose? When you lay down your head at night, do you rest peacefully knowing you are fulfilling the mission you asked to come here for?

Or do you feel rudderless, spinning in circles, bumping into one situation after the next with no clear direction of where you're going?

This is something I have struggled with myself from time to time. And I think the best advice is to tune into your soul and ask these questions: What pulls you the strongest? What do you really love? If you could do anything and money was no object, what would you do?

Asking yourself these questions can reveal a lot about your true passions and ultimately what your life purpose is. You see, I believe purpose comes from passion. And when you're living in your passion, you are living in your joy.

"Joy is but the sign that creative emotion is fulfilling its purpose."

~ Charles Du Bos

My intention is not to cause you stress if you're not certain of your purpose yet. Some people wait an entire lifetime before it is uncovered. My desire is that you begin to ask yourself these questions because this topic is about more than life purpose. It's about living "on purpose" in all you do and say and feel and think. This might help.

We've talked a bit about the "what" and the "how" part of the living on purpose, I want to bring you to the most important part of the discovery – your "why." I've found that this is the hardest part, because it requires that you go deep inside yourself to communicate with your soul.

You need to be able to strip off the opinions of others, to peel away your beliefs about what you "should" feel. Essentially, your why must come from within and can't be imposed or chosen from outside of yourself.

A fantastic book I read that really inspired me is *Start with Why*, by Simon Sinek. Although the book was written primarily for a corporate audience, I found it to be incredibly relevant to my personal life as well. It really helped me clarify my own whys as they relate not only to the way I make my living, but to how I engage with the world around me. This might help in your quest as well.

> ***"And the day came when the risk it took to remain tight in the bud was more painful than the risk it took to blossom."***
> ~ Anais Nin

As Norman Cousins said, "The sense of paralysis proceeds not so much out of the mammoth size of the problem but out of the puniness of the purpose." So, no more puny purposes. Please don't resign yourself out of fear or doubt – don't live in your limitations. Be bold, think big, because in this case, size does matter. And to me that is joyful living.

Day 30

MY DAILY AFFIRMATION

I know that I have a purpose that matters.
It guides me from deep in my soul.
My heart sets the vision.
My mind fuels the mission.
And joy is the ultimate goal.

MY DAILY ACTIVITY

THINK BIGGER: If money or your present circumstances were not an issue, what would you most want to do? What's been calling you? What's the first thing that comes to mind? Write it down. Now, get out of your mind and into your heart and describe the reason ***why*** you want to do this? Describe it in as much detail as you can. Who will you help? How would your life be different? Now list the actions you could take to move closer to the fulfilment of your purpose. The desire is there for a reason. The Universe is simply responding to your heart's whisper. Believe.

MY DAILY FREQUENCY SHIFTER

At the end of each day, rate your state of joy on this **Joy-meter** *and then make any comments or observations about your feelings during the day or about anything noteworthy that occurred. This will help you see how your joy increases during the 40 days and what "shows up" for you.*

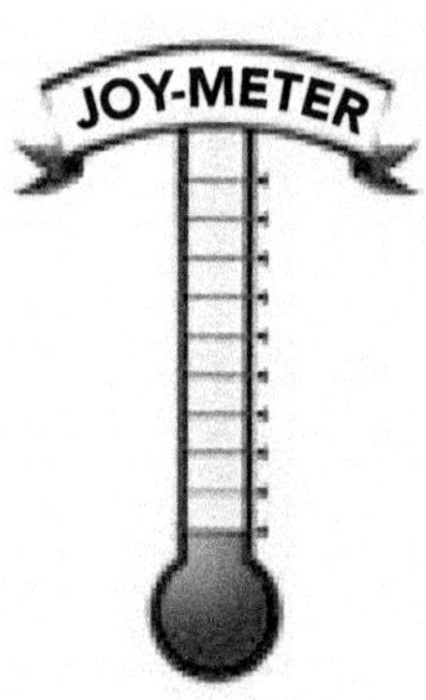

10 – Off the charts.
9 – Super amazing.
8 – Pretty blissful.
7 – Oh happy joy.
6 – I believe.
5 – I've turned the corner.
4 – I'm breathing easier.
3 – I can see the light.
2 – The clouds are lifting.
1 – I feel depressed.

NOTES

Day 30

MORE NOTES

Day 31

BE HONOURABLE

"The greatest way to live with honour in this world is to be what we pretend to be."

~ Socrates

Honouring is the foundation of harmony. In fact, American developmental biologist Bruce Lipton, says, "Frontier science has emphasized that our survival is dependent upon us to return to our aboriginal roots that stressed the belief that humans are one with nature. Aboriginal people recognize and honour the "spirits" of the air, the water, the rocks, the plants and animals and most importantly, the spiritual nature of themselves."

Hard to disagree with that. If you accept the premise that everything is connected, then it stands to reason that when we honour our environment, our birds and animals, and all peoples, then we ultimately honour ourselves.

Today's topic for joyful living is about honour – for yourself and others. And the starting place is with the self.

There is no fooling your higher self. And when you think, act, speak, and live in alignment with your core values, you radiate with honour, integrity, and ultimately with joy. You live up to yourself.

Honour is also synonymous with respect in my book – to honour someone is to show the highest respect and regard for them. And again, this first begins with you. Self-respect comes from self-love. You can't have one without the other. And as I've said before, you can't give what you don't have. So, start by looking inside and honouring yourself first.

As we discussed in Chapter 17 on accountability, honour is also about keeping your agreements. To live with honour means to keep promises to yourself and others, even when it would be easier to do otherwise – especially when it would be easier to take another path. Those critical moments in your life are what help to define your character.

"Honor isn't about making the right choices.
It's about dealing with the consequences."
~ Sophocles

Every day our honour is tested in some way. In may be in small, perhaps seemingly inconsequential ways, or in more significant ways. But the fact is, if we pay attention, we'll be aware of the tests. And how we react will be what defines our honour.

Because you are an important member of our planet's community, you are worthy of respect and honour. Please don't forget this. You are needed. Now all you have to do is live up to it. And by doing so, that is joyful living.

Day 31

MY DAILY AFFIRMATION

I honour my choices on good days and bad
as I keep my agreements with soul.
Living up to my vision of what lies ahead
I honour myself as a whole

MY DAILY ACTIVITY

CELEBRATE INTEGRITY: Think of a promise or agreement that you have made to yourself or someone else and that you've kept. It could be as simple as promising your partner to be more considerate or as challenging as quitting smoking or drinking. Now celebrate your integrity with a great big hug for yourself – I mean it. Wrap your arms around yourself and squeeze tight and remember how much you are loved.

MY DAILY FREQUENCY SHIFTER

At the end of each day, rate your state of joy on this **Joy-meter** *and then make any comments or observations about your feelings during the day or about anything noteworthy that occurred. This will help you see how your joy increases during the 40 days and what "shows up" for you.*

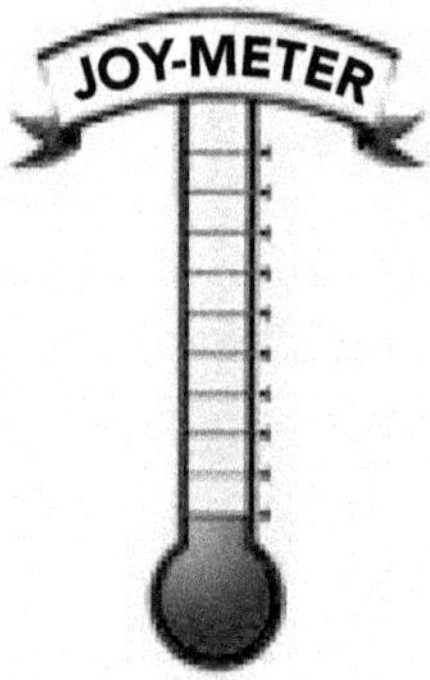

10 – Off the charts.
9 – Super amazing.
8 – Pretty blissful.
7 – Oh happy joy.
6 – I believe.
5 – I've turned the corner.
4 – I'm breathing easier.
3 – I can see the light.
2 – The clouds are lifting.
1 – I feel depressed.

NOTES

Day 31

MORE NOTES

Day 32

BE HELPFUL

"Nobody made a greater mistake than he who did nothing because he could only do a little."

~ Edmund Burke

To be helpful goes beyond being kind or being of service. It's a state of being in which you are on the look-out for opportunities to share your own life experiences with others in a way that will demonstrate our shared humanity as opposed to our differences. In a way that will be truly helpful.

From the time I was a young girl, I was an activist, fixated on making change. And I was busy organizing others to do the same. You can ask my brother about the many clubs and neighbourhood things I roped him and the other kids on the block into taking part in. And then when the sixties and early seventies came along, I soon realized I wasn't alone.

I wanted to fix so many things, that at the time I saw as "broken," that I soon began to feel frustrated and quite inadequate. I felt that I might never really make a difference. Then my dad said something that remains with me still.

He said that I didn't need to travel to a third-world country or to an impoverished village to make a difference. I didn't have to try and change everything. I only had to focus on being helpful to one person at a time – make one gesture at a time. And I could start right from my own back yard.

That propelled me into the life I have today. And if you look back at your own life, I'm sure you'll find a pivotal moment in your own experience, something that someone said or did that demonstrated what genuine helpfulness looks like. You learned from them and were perhaps inspired as well. Draw upon that.

"If you can't feed a hundred people, then feed just one."
~Mother Teresa

Sometimes the needs of the world might seem so overwhelming to you, that you begin to question how one person can really make a difference. You may say, how can I live up to the example of great people like the Dalai Lama or Gandhi or Mother Teresa?

But you see, the reality is that the energy of your helpfulness will have a ripple effect on others, far more than you can imagine. That one person you helped, will then go on to help another and in turn that person will help someone else and so on. You will have started a chain-reaction – a virus of love for humankind. So, I say, do what you can with what you have. That's what being helpful truly means. And we can all do that.

"Never doubt that a small group of thoughtful, committed citizens can change the world; indeed, it's the only thing that ever has."
~ Margaret Mead

When you live in the state of helpfulness, you see others through the lens of love instead of need. You look at people, not as being deficient or "broken" but of deserving of love and compassion. You look for opportunities to share of yourself. It's not a forced gesture. It becomes automatic and natural.

Begin by asking, "How can I make a difference in the life of this person right now, through my words or my deeds? How can I get out of my own ego and see the light in their being? How can I enrich their experience and bring more joy into their life?"

Remember, it doesn't have to be a massive thing. It could be as simple as helping them by just listening, which is one of the greatest gestures of respect and validation. As Thich Nhat Hanh said, "The most precious gift we can offer anyone is our attention."

So, my request of you, is to practice awareness of others. Look for ways to be helpful, without being asked, and without judgement or expectation. Look for ways to be their light, to be their joy until they can return to their own. For as Karl Reiland said, "In about the same degree as you are helpful, you will be happy." Always the Law of Attraction at work. And that is joyful living.

Day 32

MY DAILY AFFIRMATION

How may I help is my creed for the day
as I look for new ways to give joy.
I help one by one
knowing I have begun
to shift goodness for all to enjoy.

MY DAILY ACTIVITY

THE GIFT OF JOY: Think of someone you know who has been struggling. Reach out to them today in an unexpected way. Is there something you could do to ease their burden? Or simply give them the gifts of your time, your heart, your caring. Give them the gift of joy.

MY DAILY FREQUENCY SHIFTER

At the end of each day, rate your state of joy on this **Joy-meter** *and then make any comments or observations about your feelings during the day or about anything noteworthy that occurred. This will help you see how your joy increases during the 40 days and what "shows up" for you.*

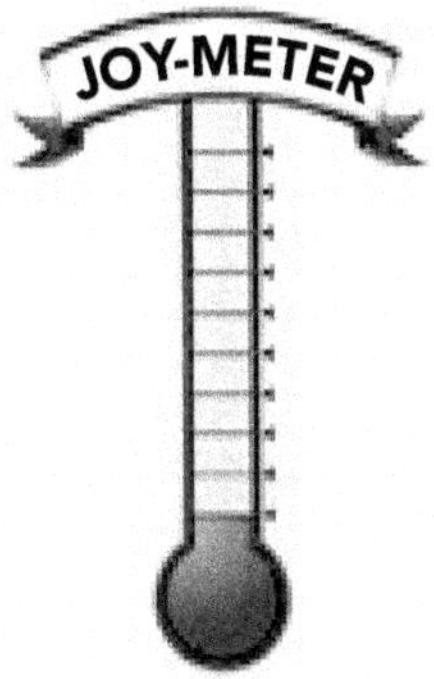

10 – Off the charts.
9 – Super amazing.
8 – Pretty blissful.
7 – Oh happy joy.
6 – I believe.
5 – I've turned the corner.
4 – I'm breathing easier.
3 – I can see the light.
2 – The clouds are lifting.
1 – I feel depressed.

NOTES

Day 32

Day 33

BE THOUGHTFUL

"Ancient spiritual traditions remind us that in each moment of the day, we make the choices that either affirm or deny our lives. Every second we choose to nourish ourselves in a way that supports or depletes our lives; to breathe deep and life-affirming breaths or shallow, life-denying ones; and to think and speak about other people in a manner that is honoring or dishonoring."

~ Gregg Braden

Like the air you breathe and the music you listen to, the words you speak are equally important to the joy you experience in life.

It's so easy to get caught up in the conversation of what's wrong with the world, with the violence, the injustice, the fear.

We allow our conversations to revolve around what other people are doing or buying or who they're with and how they behave. We use other people as a barometer to compare ourselves. And when we put them down, or gossip about them, we believe it will make us feel better. But in fact, it has the opposite effect. It steals our joy.

You see when you think and speak in negative ways about yourselves or others, you attract negative energy into your life, lower your frequency, and deplete your life.

Many of us probably do this without even being aware we are. After all, we're likely modelling this behavior after family or our peers. So, I ask you now to shift your focus away from negative inner dialogue and instead onto life-affirming language.

"If we understood the power of our thoughts, we would guard them more closely. If we understood the awesome power of our words, we would prefer silence to almost anything negative. In our thoughts and words, we create our own weaknesses and our own strengths. Our limitations and joys begin in our hearts. We can always replace negative with positive."

~ Betty Eadie

Start by catching yourself every time you start to go down that familiar path of negative self-talk, gossip, or complaining. Remember when you talk down to yourself, you are telling yourself you are not worthy. And when you complain, you are just seeing yourself as a victim. And when you gossip, you are not only judging others, but you are judging yourself as well. None of these thoughts are empowering. They will just keep you stuck in a place that you are trying to get away from.

I want to talk for a minute about the power of words. In the book *Angel Words*, written by Doreen and Grant Virtue, they talk about the vibrational patterns of positive and negative words. In fact, they were able to graph the vibration of words with amazing results.

"Raise your words, not your voice.
It is rain that grows flowers, not thunder."
~ Rumi

The positive words looked angelic and beautiful whereas the negative words were dark and ominous. Much like in the work that Dr. Emoto did with water molecules that I talked about in Chapter 9, there is ample scientific evidence that the words we use and the thoughts we think have energy and can have an impact on our lives and the lives of others.

When you catch yourself saying something negative out loud or even to yourself, start saying, "Stop, cancel, delete." This will interrupt the pattern of negativity and tell the Universe you don't want more of the same. Then immediately shift your thinking into a positive dialogue. You'll find yourself becoming more calm and peaceful in the process. And you'll discover more positive people and things showing up for you.

"The words you speak become the house you live in."
~ Hafiz

So today as you practice mindfulness about your thoughts and words, remember that your spirit is being nourished as you honour yourself with this positive way of communicating to yourself and others. And that is joyful living.

Day 33

MY DAILY AFFIRMATION

I listen to the words I choose
and catch the ones that serve us.
The ones that heal are those most real.
The others have no purpose.

MY DAILY ACTIVITY

WORD CATCHING: Do your best today to catch yourself when you use low-energy words like "can't," "demand," "bad," "hate," "shut-up." Or life-defeating phrases like "it's so hard." "I'm tired," "I can't afford it," or "I never get a break." Replace them with high vibrational words like "love," "comfort," "good," and "peaceful." And use life-affirming, phrases like "I am grateful," "I feel wonderful," "I choose not to buy that now," or "All is well." Gradually, you'll find that these more positive words and phrases will dominate your vocabulary and will shift the energy of people around you.

MY DAILY FREQUENCY SHIFTER

At the end of each day, rate your state of joy on this **Joy-meter** *and then make any comments or observations about your feelings during the day or about anything noteworthy that occurred. This will help you see how your joy increases during the 40 days and what "shows up" for you.*

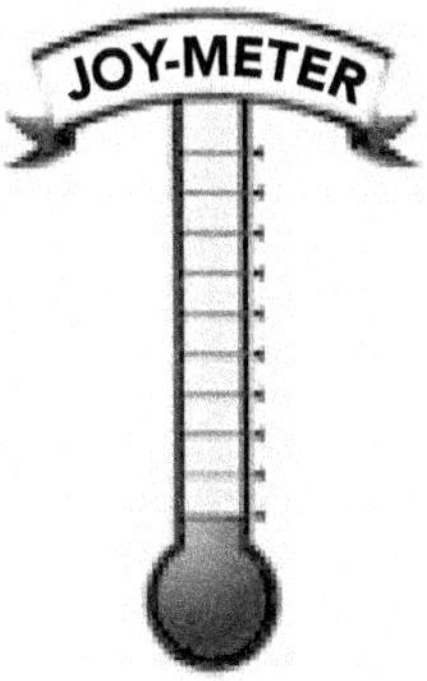

10 – Off the charts.
9 – Super amazing.
8 – Pretty blissful.
7 – Oh happy joy.
6 – I believe.
5 – I've turned the corner.
4 – I'm breathing easier.
3 – I can see the light.
2 – The clouds are lifting.
1 – I feel depressed.

NOTES

Day 33

Day 34

BE TRUTHFUL

"If you do not tell the truth about yourself you cannot tell it about other people."

~ Virginia Woolf

Truthfulness – another important practice for living a more joyful life. Telling the truth. Your own truth. And telling the truth to others.

Truthfulness is likely one of the most challenging practices. Every day, we tell "little white lies" to ourselves and others. Sometimes we tell even bigger ones.

Perhaps it's to spare the feelings of someone or as a way to rationalize something we've done. But at our soul level, we know the truth and yet we still choose to conceal it. Then we feel ashamed – one of the most toxic emotions we can have and one that lowers our vibration the most.

"The way of peace is the way of truth. Truthfulness is even more important than peacefulness."
~ Mahatma Gandhi

To me, the topic of truthfulness is about knowing yourself – understanding what you stand for and what you hold to be true for yourself. Being discerning. Not allowing others to influence what you think. It's about showing up as you really are and believing that you're good enough.

When you practice truthfulness on a daily basis, you become more empowered. You don't have to exaggerate or deceive to impress others. When you look in the mirror, you like what you see. And when you are confident in your truthfulness, you become more appealing to others. They can see the real you and know they can trust what they see.

"The truth is like a lion. You don't have to defend it. Let it loose. It will defend itself."
~ St. Augustine

So, stop trying to be someone you're not. Dig deep down to your soul and uncover the real you. Show it proudly. It's good enough. And that is joyful living.

Day 34

MY DAILY AFFIRMATION

As I look deep down inside
to find my truth within,
I choose to show it proudly now
and love in my own skin.

MY DAILY ACTIVITY

TRUTH JOURNAL: Make a list of the positive qualities you possess and another list of those that you would like to change. Be honest with yourself. Awareness is always the first step. Celebrate your honesty by acknowledging both.

MY DAILY FREQUENCY SHIFTER

At the end of each day, rate your state of joy on this **Joy-meter** *and then make any comments or observations about your feelings during the day or about anything noteworthy that occurred. This will help you see how your joy increases during the 40 days and what "shows up" for you.*

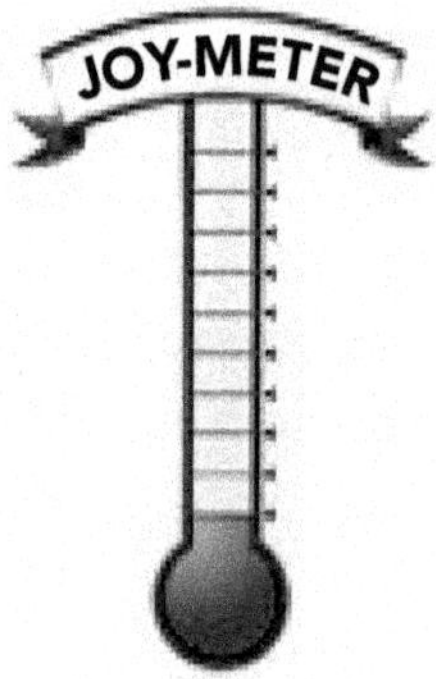

10 – Off the charts.
9 – Super amazing.
8 – Pretty blissful.
7 – Oh happy joy.
6 – I believe.
5 – I've turned the corner.
4 – I'm breathing easier.
3 – I can see the light.
2 – The clouds are lifting.
1 – I feel depressed.

NOTES

Day 34

MORE NOTES

Day 35

BE HUMBLE

"Humility does not mean thinking less of yourself than of other people, nor does it mean having a low opinion of your own gifts. It means freedom from thinking about yourself at all."

~ William Temple

There is likely no greater selfless gesture than to completely indulge in the presence of another human being without giving a second thought to what that person might think of you. And in that act of humility, you are enabling the other person to be seen and heard without condition. In my opinion, that is the greatest service of all and one that ultimately brings joy to the spirit and to the world.

It's not an easy thing to do, however. We are conditioned from an early age to be somewhat self-centered. And the New Age movement that began to explode throughout the sixties made it o.k. to think about yourself first. Getting to know the inner child etc. etc. As a product of the sixties, I think sometimes we missed the point. Let me explain what I mean.

"All streams flow to the sea because it is lower than they are. Humility gives it its power."

~ Lao-Tzu

I believe whole-heartedly in the importance of self-care – to be unapologetic about ridding yourself of past blame, shame, and baggage. To continue to explore how you feel and to question your beliefs, which ultimately create your reality. That's your responsibility. But not at the expense of another human being.

I remember years ago, when I was first married to my son's father, we were on a road trip to the mountains with two other couples. Both of the other couples were heavily into transcendental meditation and it took about thirty minutes to figure out the driving arrangements so that one person could drive and the others could meditate. We ended up taking two cars.

I remember at the time thinking how insensitive these people were to the needs of those of us who weren't familiar with TM. They were so involved in self and attached to the routine feeding of their enlightenment that they did not notice others. I felt there was no respect and therefore no humility.

"Humility is not denying your strengths.
Humility is about being honest about your weaknesses."
~ Rick Warren

I now realize that I was making a judgement. And because judgements stem from ego, I was no different than them. I was so attached to my own beliefs about how they should or should not behave that I missed the opportunity to simply relax, enjoy the quiet and respect their choice.

That experience has stayed with me over all these years as a reminder to refrain from "preaching" my own philosophies or beliefs to others, but instead, to share when appropriate – always respecting that other people have their own experiences that shape their beliefs. And to be humble in the presence of others – to let my ego take a back seat to my higher self.

"Humility is the solid foundation of all virtues."
~ Confucius

Over the years I have also been blessed to witness great acts of grace from people who humbly shared what little they had and whose simple gestures of love and humility brought out the best in all who witnessed their acts of respect, consideration, and love. To me that's the point. That's service through humility, allowing true joy to be witnessed for all to be elevated by.

Think about the great men and women of humility who have walked this earth and some who still do. People like Jesus, Buddha, Gandhi, Mother Teresa and the Dalai Lama. What overwhelming peace and joy people have experienced by merely being in their presence. You see, there's a positive energetic impact on your body, mind, and spirit when you witness acts of humility and kindness. You feel better and are temporarily shifted into a higher frequency. Now, if you can stay in that frequency and commit to following their example, then you help shift the energy of people you interact with. And that's how we begin to shift the frequency of the world – one person at a time.

Today I hope you will engage fully with the world around you without judgement or expectation. Practice humility and be at peace. And that is joyful living.

Day 35

MY DAILY AFFIRMATION

I listen intently, no judgements from me
as my heart hears the story of others.
For I know as I stand here
with scars of my own
I could easily resemble another.

MY DAILY ACTIVITY

JUDGEMENT RELEASE: Count how many times today you think, speak, or act in a way that is judgemental of yourself or others. Then promise to reduce the number tomorrow and then the next day and the next day. Gradually, with mindfulness, you will begin to release the ego's desire to judge and find yourself living more joyfully with humility.

MY DAILY FREQUENCY SHIFTER

At the end of each day, rate your state of joy on this **Joy-meter** *and then make any comments or observations about your feelings during the day or about anything noteworthy that occurred. This will help you see how your joy increases during the 40 days and what "shows up" for you.*

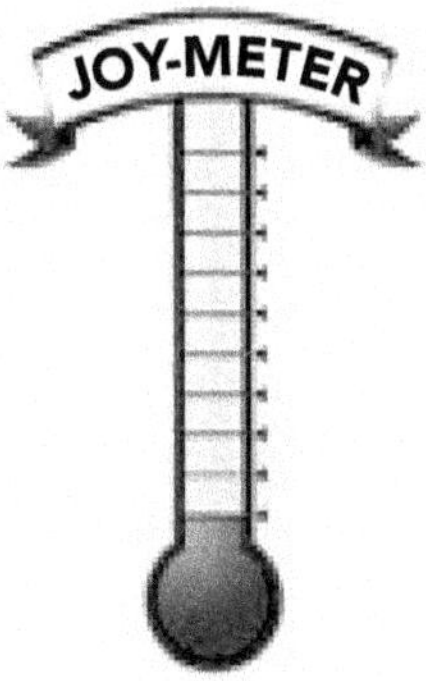

10 – Off the charts.
9 – Super amazing.
8 – Pretty blissful.
7 – Oh happy joy.
6 – I believe.
5 – I've turned the corner.
4 – I'm breathing easier.
3 – I can see the light.
2 – The clouds are lifting.
1 – I feel depressed.

NOTES

____

____

____

____

____

____

____

____

____

____

____

Day 36

BE CONNECTED

"We are here to awaken from the illusion of our separateness."

~ Thich Nhat Hanh

Often, when we experience difficult times in our lives, it's easy to feel that we're all alone – that no one will understand. You may have even convinced yourself that no one cares. And when that happens, you have drifted into an isolation of spirit.

As challenging as it may be to think otherwise, it's at this very time that you must quiet your troubled mind so that you can hear the whispers as other souls encourage you.

If you believe as I do, that every living thing has energy and that we live in an inter-connected universe, then as human beings we are also connected in spirit.

As scientist Neil deGrasse Tyson says, "We are all connected. To each other, biologically. To the earth, chemically. To the rest of the universe, atomically."

This means that you are never alone because we are all here to be of service to one another. For what we do for someone else, comes back to us. Science understands this principle. So do the scriptures. Simply put, you matter.

"For listening to the stories of others, not to their precautions or personal commandments, is a kind of water that breaks the fever of our isolation. If we listen closely enough, we are soothed into remembering our common name."

~Mark Nepo

Throughout this book, I have underscored how your beliefs, thoughts, words, and actions impact and define your reality. And because we are all connected, that means you will attract those people into your life who can be of the most service to you and you to them. You just may not always recognize their significance at the time.

I'd like to share an example from my own life. Back in the late 1980s I was diagnosed with multiple sclerosis. Because of my belief system at the time and reinforced by genuine fear and concern from friends and family, I believed that I would ultimately end up in a wheelchair. And because there was little treatment at that time and made painfully clear to me - no cure, it was suggested that I plan my life in accordance with these expectations and new limitations.

However, after my divorce, and then because of three significant exacerbations, I noticed that there was a definite correlation between how I was thinking and living and the people I was attracting into my life. They were, in fact, the ones who mirrored back to me how I was living – my biggest teachers of what I no longer wished to be.

"It is easy to believe we are each waves and forget we are also the ocean."
~ Jon J. Muth

I was then referred to a massage therapist who would be the biggest catalyst for change in my life up to that point. As I began to feel physically better, I began to feel better emotionally as well. And as my emotional balance improved, then my physical health continued to improve.

I became interested in other healing modalities and started to explore metaphysics. As I was introduced to new people, who miraculously appeared in my life, I was able to identify the mirror images a little faster and soon realized they were mirroring my "new way" of being.

By listening to my body, I am getting better at discerning which people are in my life to show me the paths to avoid and which can open doors to my greatest joy. But like everything else, this is a process. Many times, I am not able to understand the significance of the connection until later. But by trusting my body, I am, at least, aware enough to take notice.

"Like birds flying in a V,
when we feel the presence of others moving
alongside of us, there is little we cannot accomplish."
~ Madisyn Taylor

I invite you to take notice without judgement, but instead with discernment on what feels good and what does not. People representing both feelings will find their way to you. And even when you choose to follow the path that doesn't feel good, there is still value from that experience. This is simply another gift of life-learning made possible because of a connection you made. That doesn't make anyone bad or the experience worthless. You attracted them and it into reality for a purpose. Be grateful, for whether you can appreciate it now or not, that is joyful living.

Day 36

MY DAILY AFFIRMATION

I'm not alone, I do belong
to other souls beloved.
Our paths are different but at the core
We know we're all connected.

MY DAILY ACTIVITY

JOIN IN: Think of a group of like-minded people that you would like to join or start in the next thirty days. If you're already part of a group, then expand your community by stretching yourself to look for more diversity in your life. Connect, connect, connect.

MY DAILY FREQUENCY SHIFTER

At the end of each day, rate your state of joy on this **Joy-meter** *and then make any comments or observations about your feelings during the day or about anything noteworthy that occurred. This will help you see how your joy increases during the 40 days and what "shows up" for you.*

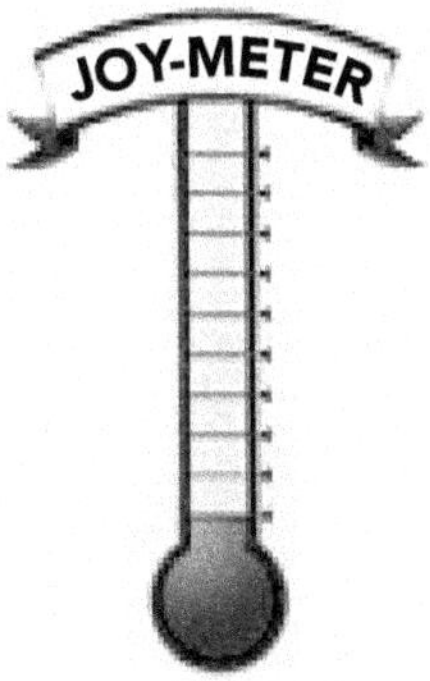

10 – Off the charts.
9 – Super amazing.
8 – Pretty blissful.
7 – Oh happy joy.
6 – I believe.
5 – I've turned the corner.
4 – I'm breathing easier.
3 – I can see the light.
2 – The clouds are lifting.
1 – I feel depressed.

NOTES

Day 36

Day 37

BE LIGHT-HEARTED

"Light-heartedness is the closest earthly condition to heaven."

~ Doreen Virtue

Sometimes, we can just take ourselves and life itself a little bit too seriously. We get caught up in the perceived drama of everyday happenings, often making more out of a situation than it deserves. It's all about perspective. And we can get really stuck in that spiral if we're not mindful. We've all done it.

So, today's theme is all about giving yourself permission to laugh rather than curse when you bang your knee against the coffee table and to smile instead of frown when your bag of groceries breaks and your oranges go rolling across the parking lot. It's a healthier response for your body and mind.

Take for example the personal story of Norman Cousins, the American author, professor, and political journalist, who was diagnosed with a severe inflammatory disease and was not expected to recover. In constant pain, he decided to try a different approach to healing. He chose laughter. He watched hours of funny movies and listened to funny stories. With just ten minutes of laughter, he reported that he could have two hours of pain-free sleep. As Cousins said, "Laughter is just inner jogging."

Scientists and other experts agree that laughter is a legitimate form of therapy as can be seen by the many children's hospitals and wellness centres that have introduced laughter therapy as a respected addition to their therapeutic tool box.

"God is a comedian playing to an audience too afraid to laugh."

~Voltaire

Researchers have found that laughter helps to lower blood glucose-levels for Type 2 diabetes as well as for immune system and cardiovascular health, not to mention the impact on stress reduction. So, the old saying that laughter is the best medicine is no longer just something we say – it's backed by science.

I am such a big believer in the power of humour to heal. I've experienced it in my own lifetime and time again have watched close family families benefit from humour when dealing with illness and other difficult issues.

"At the height of laughter, the universe is flung into a kaleidoscope of new possibilities."
~Jean Houston

Laughter can bring us closer together and elevate the collective energy of the room. In my opinion, there is nothing better than a good belly laugh to ease stress and return light to your heart. You see, joy cannot exist when there is stress, and therefore stress cannot exist when there is joy. Please choose joy as your natural state of being.

Today, I ask you to look for more opportunities to laugh – at yourself, at situations, and at some of the oddities of life (plenty of fodder in this department). And as you feel the rush of endorphins that fill your body, exhale and smile. For that is joyful living.

Day 37

MY DAILY AFFIRMATION

Today I laugh with all my heart
to ease my stress and worry.
The air feels light,
with grip less tight
and joy says, "What's the hurry?"

MY DAILY ACTIVITY

LAUGH AT YOURSELF: Do or wear something out of the ordinary today. Something that is totally ridiculous and will make you laugh out loud. If you are in a situation where you can't publicly look silly, then wear some silly underwear or something that only you will know about. Silent smiles are good until you get home and then let it all hang out.

MY DAILY FREQUENCY SHIFTER

At the end of each day, rate your state of joy on this ***Joy-meter*** *and then make any comments or observations about your feelings during the day or about anything noteworthy that occurred. This will help you see how your joy increases during the 40 days and what "shows up" for you.*

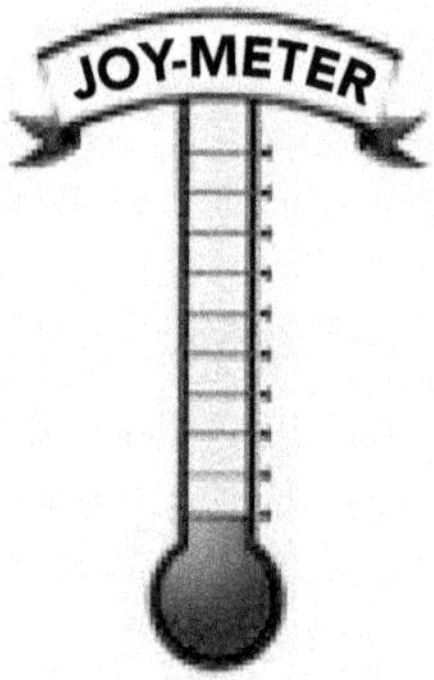

10 – Off the charts.
9 – Super amazing.
8 – Pretty blissful.
7 – Oh happy joy.
6 – I believe.
5 – I've turned the corner.
4 – I'm breathing easier.
3 – I can see the light.
2 – The clouds are lifting.
1 – I feel depressed.

NOTES

Day 37

MORE NOTES

Day 38

BE PLEASURE

"There is a pleasure in the pathless woods,
there is a rapture in the lonely shore,
there is society where none intrudes,
by the deep sea, and music in its roar;
I love not Man the less, but Nature more."

~ Lord Byron

Make today about self-nurturing. And if you can, do it outside, for that is the place where you will feel the most alive and most connected with your soul. If it's summer and you can find some grass, take off your shoes, and walk barefoot. Feel the earth's energy vibrate through your body. Remember to hug a tree. Feel your senses come alive. Delight in this simple pleasure.

If not, then just go outside and breathe deeply. Your lungs will feel the pleasure of crisp freshness. My favourite time to do this is first thing in the morning when the world still feels untouched and new – to me, that's when the air is sweetest.

Today is about letting your senses come alive. Book a massage or facial. Take a bubble bath, wear clothing that feels sensuous to the skin, eat foods that are comforting and luxurious. Have breakfast in bed while reading a book. Or just lie in silence. Be pleasure.

And please, please, please don't for one minute feel guilty about taking time for yourself. This is so essential for your mental and physical health as well as your spiritual growth. Remember you deserve all this world has to offer and all you desire. Joy is your birthright, so indulge with gusto.

"There is a connection between self-nurturing and self-respect."

~ Julia Cameron

One of my favourite things to do when I need some time to myself without distraction or responsibility, is to read. I love reading and always have. I find that's where my imagination comes alive and often when my best ideas are born. Do you have a favourite chair in a favourite room to do this? Pour yourself a nice cup of tea and maybe some yummy cookies and nestle in for an adventure. Or if your house is too hectic, escape to a coffee shop, library, or park.

Maybe pleasure to you is watching a good movie with a big bowl of popcorn. I'm with you on that one. Or maybe you like to bake, sew, sing, draw, dance, or write – it's your way of nurturing your inner expressive self – your inner child.

The point is that whatever you choose to do today, it should be just about you. And if you can't devote the entire day to it, then carve out at least thirty minutes to an hour of time just for yourself. And then keep up the habit – try for a bit of time every day just for you. It's important. You're important. You'll not only be validating your own worth, but you will also be showing others how you wish to be considered. And if you have children, please remember that you are not being selfish – just the opposite. You are teaching them how to treat themselves and others.

However you choose to experience pleasure today is okay – it's about you feeling worthy and at peace. And that is joyful living.

Day 38

MY DAILY AFFIRMATION

To have an indulgence – no reason at all
is to practice the gift of receiving.
I'll look for a way
to delight this new day
I'm pleased in myself for believing.

MY DAILY ACTIVITY

IT'S PAMPER TIME: Today's activity is a fun one. Just pamper yourself. Have a massage, take a nature walk, or have a salt bath to heal your body and spirit. The important thing is to do something soothing and pampering for yourself today without reservation or guilt. You are worthy of pleasure.

MY DAILY FREQUENCY SHIFTER

At the end of each day, rate your state of joy on this **Joy-meter** *and then make any comments or observations about your feelings during the day or about anything noteworthy that occurred. This will help you see how your joy increases during the 40 days and what "shows up" for you.*

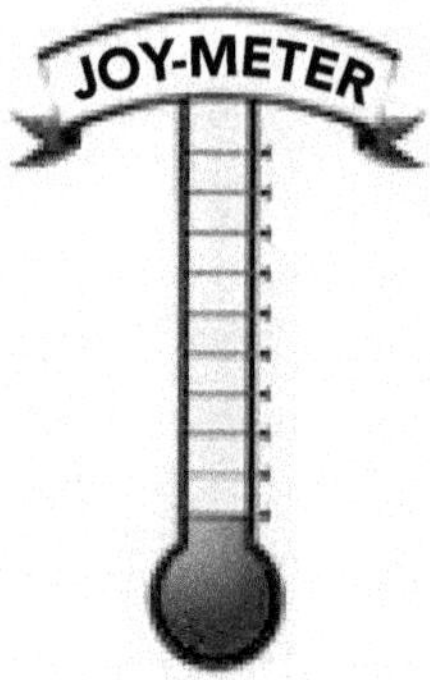

10 – Off the charts.
9 – Super amazing.
8 – Pretty blissful.
7 – Oh happy joy.
6 – I believe.
5 – I've turned the corner.
4 – I'm breathing easier.
3 – I can see the light.
2 – The clouds are lifting.
1 – I feel depressed.

NOTES

MORE NOTES

Day 39

BE IN REVERENCE

"Always and in everything let there be reverence."

~ Confucius

It always amazes me when I read a quote that was written so long ago, like the one from Confucius for this chapter. These words are as relevant today as when they were written, perhaps even more so.

Confucius, who was China's most famous teacher, philosopher, and political theorist, lived from 551-479 BC and coined so many sayings that he may indeed be one of the most quoted persons in history. I particularly love this quote and with today's theme of reverence, for the second-to-last day of your joy experience, I am happy to share it with you.

So, let's look at this quote. *"Always and in everything let there be reverence."* So, what does this mean in today's age? Adopting a total commitment to loving everything always. But how can you love everything? What about people who have wronged you? What about the "ugly" side of life? How can you revere that?

Tough questions. But if you follow the philosophy that everything in life is connected and that you are simply experiencing people and things that you have co-created, then it is easier to acknowledge that they have a purpose – even if you're not exactly sure quite yet what that purpose is. Accept, love, and revere them anyway, for they are part of your story. I believe Confucius understood this well.

"Walk as if you are kissing the Earth with your feet."
~ Thich Nhat Hanh

Confucius and so many other wise teachers from history understood that everything in life is sacred. And to show reverence is to show respect – to show love. And once you replace complaining and blame with appreciation and acceptance, you'll feel more reverence towards yourself. That, in turn, will alter what you see and experience. As Wayne Dyer said, "When you change the way you look at things, the things you look at change." You see, reverence starts from within.

I firmly believe that if more people were to find the hush of reverence in their everyday experience, stress levels would come down, there would be fewer illnesses and premature deaths, and we would move closer to living in a more peaceful and sustainable world. So today, revere life and everything in it. It is of your creation and is yours to love. And that is joyful living.

Day 39

MY DAILY AFFIRMATION

I accept and revere all the things in my life.
All sacred because they exist.
For life's never random.
There are no mistakes.
I am grateful I do not resist.

MY DAILY ACTIVITY

SACRED RITUAL: Find some quiet time, preferably first thing in the morning or in the evening to create a sacred ritual just for yourself. Light candles, burn incense, or diffuse essential oils. If you have crystals or stones you want to use, then hold them. Tranquil music is nice. With eyes open, and without judgement, slowly look around giving thanks for everything you see.

MY DAILY FREQUENCY SHIFTER

At the end of each day, rate your state of joy on this ***Joy-meter*** *and then make any comments or observations about your feelings during the day or about anything noteworthy that occurred. This will help you see how your joy increases during the 40 days and what "shows up" for you.*

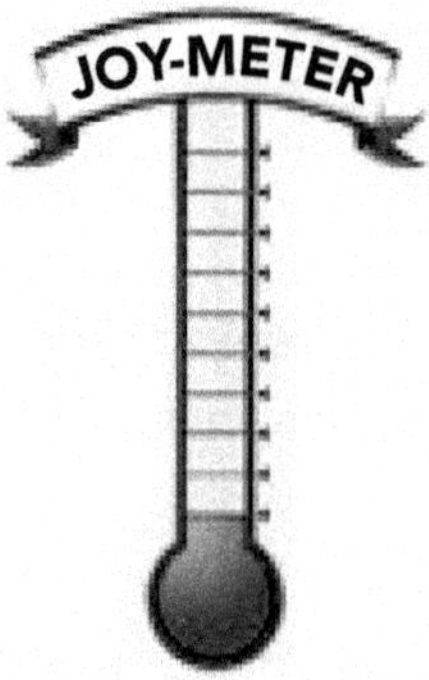

10 – Off the charts.
9 – Super amazing.
8 – Pretty blissful.
7 – Oh happy joy.
6 – I believe.
5 – I've turned the corner.
4 – I'm breathing easier.
3 – I can see the light.
2 – The clouds are lifting.
1 – I feel depressed.

NOTES

MORE NOTES

Day 40

BE ALIGNED

"I am in the right place,
at the right time,
doing the right thing."

~ Louise L. Hay

Congratulations. You did it. Today is the last day of your 40-Day Joy Experience. I hope you've enjoyed the journey and will continue to repeat this program from time to time or refer back to specific chapters for a "tune-up" when you feel the need.

I've saved the best for last – or at least I believe it's the most important subject to complete our time together as it combines so many of the other thirty-nine daily themes.

You hear a lot these days about "living in alignment" – with your soul's desire and your life purpose. Confused? Feeling a bit lost? If so, I can relate. I was too.

First of all, I don't claim to be an expert on this subject. What I've learned about alignment has come from some of my trusted advisors and spiritual teachers and through reading and listening to those I consider respected sources like Abraham-Hicks, Wayne Dyer, and others. I'm still learning, and I encourage you to do the same. What I'm about to share is from where I stand now.

So much of what I read in the past had to do with aligning with my life-purpose. So, I became fixated on trying to figure that out. But what if you're not sure? Many aren't.

I found I was putting so much pressure on myself, trying to figure out in my head what my life purpose was – what I was supposed to "do" that I began to feel like a failure when I couldn't figure it out. You see alignment is an inner thing, not something you think your way through. You must "feel" your way into it. I realized I was viewing alignment in a very limited way.

"Your greatest challenge is to not be distracted by that which happens in front of you, or is pulling on you or calling to you, but instead to find your center and magnetize to yourself all those things that are in alignment with your inner being."
~ Sanaya Roman

You see, from what I understand now, you and I are both physical and spiritual beings and our souls are just a part of Source Energy – our origin, and we are always connected to it. Source Energy is loving, peaceful, and joyful. That's our natural state of being.

So, when we are living in alignment with our souls, we feel good and at peace and when we aren't living in alignment, we feel bad. Kind of simple but not really. Let me explain.

Let's say you are in a job you don't like, and you want to change careers. Or you don't earn enough money to cover your monthly bills, so you want more money. Or you are retired and bored and would like something meaningful to do with your time – so you send your desires out as a vibration from your soul.

But what often happens is that when those desires don't manifest right away, you feel upset or disbelieving. You feel bad.

The problem is that because of your attachment to old beliefs or doubt or feelings of unworthiness, you haven't allowed yourself to catch up to the new vision you have of yourself at the soul level. You are basically constricting the flow.

So, what's the solution? Feel good first. Let the emotions of belief, love, acceptance, peace, and joy elevate your vibrational frequency so that you allow the expansion of your desires – you "allow" the flow.

"Let your alignment with Well-Being be first and foremost and let everything else be secondary. And not only will you have an eternally joyous journey, but everything you have ever imagined will flow effortlessly into your experience."

~ Abraham-Hicks

So, my beloved reader, please know that you have the right to desire. And your desires can be fulfilled. Go within, connect with your soul, and trust your feelings. And don't look back. And that, my friend, is joyful living at its most glorious!

Day 40

MY DAILY AFFIRMATION

I move closer to my core
and live from heart and soul.
I am aligned with love and joy
I know it to be so.

MY DAILY ACTIVITY

FIND YOUR SOUL SONG: Today you're going to hum. Not only has research shown the many health benefits of humming to clear sinuses, help with heart-health, calm the nervous system and reduce stress, but humming is a powerful "sound" medicine for the spirit. Either hum along to peaceful music you have playing or simply make up your own tune to hum to. The vibrations in your throat will record your very own soul song for you to recall whenever you need a reminder that you are divine. YOU ARE JOY.

MY DAILY FREQUENCY SHIFTER

At the end of each day, rate your state of joy on this ***Joy-meter*** *and then make any comments or observations about your feelings during the day or about anything noteworthy that occurred. This will help you see how your joy increases during the 40 days and what "shows up" for you.*

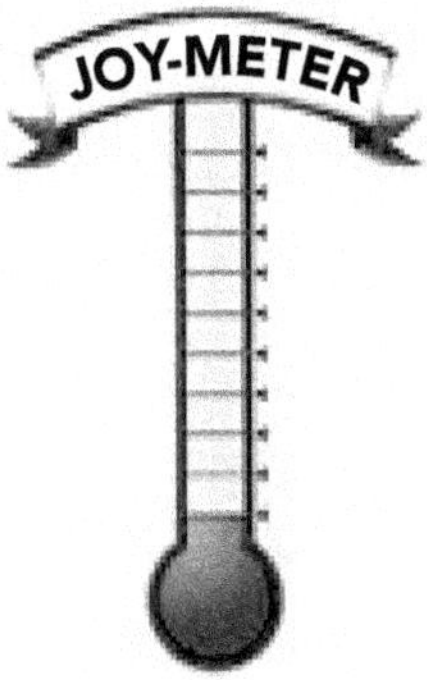

10 – Off the charts.
9 – Super amazing.
8 – Pretty blissful.
7 – Oh happy joy.
6 – I believe.
5 – I've turned the corner.
4 – I'm breathing easier.
3 – I can see the light.
2 – The clouds are lifting.
1 – I feel depressed.

NOTES

Parting Words

Joy is your birthright. But it's also your choice whether you decide to live there or not. It all depends on how you see the world.

For starters, I believe life doesn't have to be hard and that our planet is actually overflowing with abundance. In fact, for the first time in history, humanity is doing so much more with so much less. There's enough for everyone. There really are no limits –everything and anything is possible, providing we have the will.

I also believe that we are all here to make a difference – to leave the world in a better place than when we arrived. And that when we connect with one another, with shared values and common goals, well that's when the magic happens.

People from every corner of the globe are ready and waiting to be liberated from self-imposed suffering – hungry for a diet of acceptance, empowerment, and generosity of spirit. And as more of us remember our joy and embrace the power of our hearts, we move closer to creating a more equitable world.

We are the ones who will fuel the moral revival that is taking place in business and communities today. We are the ones who will create the new paradigm for true joy and abundance on our planet. Join the joyful movement – be a catalyst. Be the joy!

In Gratitude

I started this book in the spring of 2015 as a short – "7-Step Plan for Creating Joy" and soon realized that concept was too limiting and quite frankly, didn't feel very authentic. I decided to let go, be vulnerable, and trust Spirit to guide the approach and content. You are holding the end result.

In the fall of 2015 I published the *40-Day Being Joy* card deck while I worked on completing this book and workshop series. Many thanks to Meghan Delnea of Delnea Designs for the brilliant work she did in the design of the cards and book jacket. And thanks to everyone who purchased cards for themselves and for gifts. I am grateful for your continued support. I would also like to thank Morganne Pickering of Wise Women for her assistance in early book edits and to Friesen Press for your amazing resources.

Thank you to all those authors and teachers – some whom I know personally and others who I know only through their written words. You have all guided me in your own way – showing up at the exactly the right moment that I needed your insight.

And I would not be where I am today without the love and support of my family to whom I feel more connected than they will ever realize. I want to especially pay tribute to all those who came before me – my parents, grandparents, and my ancient ancestors – thank you for paving the way for my exploration and for showing me how to tap into the collective wisdom of the ages. These are gifts I will always cherish and promise to put to good use in service throughout my lifetime. Thank you.

Gloria

Other Products

The Being Joy™ cards are a convenient companion to reinforce the daily themes from this book.

To begin, I recommend using your cards in chronological order, in conjunction with the book, starting with Card #1 for Day #1 and then working with each card for a full day before moving onto the next day.

Then repeat again for another month, or blow your intention into the deck, asking for a card that will guide your thoughts and feelings for the day. Shuffle and then stop when you feel guided to or when a card "jumps" from the deck. For best results, read the card's daily affirmation several times throughout the day.

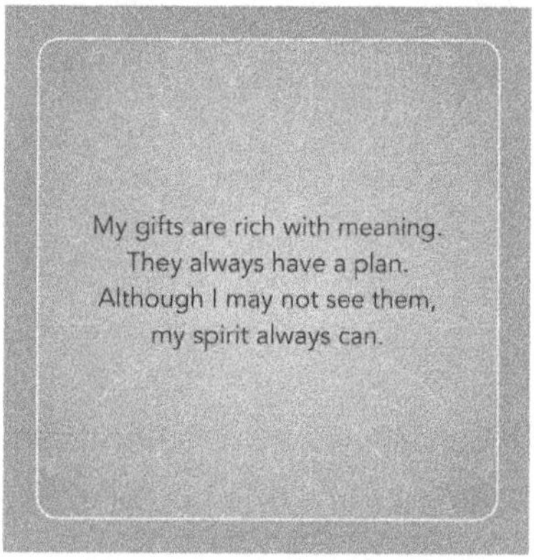

My gifts are rich with meaning.
They always have a plan.
Although I may not see them,
my spirit always can.

For pricing and to order cards, additional books or to inquire about the Being Joy workshop series, email gloria@beingjoy.ca or call (250) 248-5544. Wholesale inquiries welcome.

Customer reviews

"I have a set of the Being Joy cards and I love them. Every morning I shuffle the deck to see which inspiring card helps me set my intentions for the day. Thanks so much Gloria Stewart for sharing them with me." – **Barbara N.**

"Obviously this creation came from a heart of love and I feel it in each word I read and take into my heart. I choose a new card each day, read the message and truly meditate on the thoughts. This stays with me throughout my day and the message helps lift my spirits and move me forward. I truly recommend "Being Joy" cards as a highly inspirational way to start the day and I am grateful for the blessing of this tool." – **Margo C.**

"I love the Being Joy cards.... they give me a focus every day...something to reflect on and aspire to. The gifts I receive from the 40 days of Being Joy cards is realizing and appreciating all the Joy that is around me in this very hectic world... thank you." – **Shian P.**

"When Gloria showed me her Being Joy card set I wanted to share it with friends. And I did. Pulling a card for inspiration and intent for the day, helps friends start their day with more joy. The artwork, the packaging, and affordable price make a Being Joy card set an ideal gift. I look forward to sharing the companion book with friends."– **Cathi E.**

About the Author

Gloria Stewart is a Joy and Abundance Activist who helps individuals and organizations expand their prosperity by moving beyond survival and into joyous thriving. Having spent more than thirty years as a successful business owner helping social-purpose organizations raise millions of dollars for causes that improve the wellbeing of individuals and communities, she has observed that when people combine purpose with passion, their joy expands. And by operating in the high vibration of joy energy, a person's emotional, mental, and physical health also improves, allowing abundance to be more readily available. In addition to continuing her work in the social-purpose sector, Gloria conducts a variety of Being Joy workshops, retreats and personal sessions as a Joy and Abundance facilitator and certified Soul Coach. She makes her home on beautiful Vancouver Island, British Columbia.

CPSIA information can be obtained
at www.ICGtesting.com
Printed in the USA
LVHW040713291118
598577LV00002B/2

9 781525 534867